Classroom Go-To Guides

The Common Core in Grades 4–6: Top Nonfiction Titles from School Library Journal *and* The Horn Book Magazine, edited by Roger Sutton and Daryl Grabarek, 2014.

The Common Core in Grades K–3: Top Nonfiction Titles from School Library Journal *and* The Horn Book Magazine, edited by Roger Sutton and Daryl Grabarek, 2014.

The Common Core in Grades K–3

The Common Core in Grades K–3

Top Nonfiction Titles from
School Library Journal and
The Horn Book Magazine

Edited by
Roger Sutton
Daryl Grabarek

ROWMAN & LITTLEFIELD
Lanham • Boulder • New York • Toronto • Plymouth, UK

Published by Rowman & Littlefield
4501 Forbes Boulevard, Suite 200, Lanham, Maryland 20706
www.rowman.com

10 Thornbury Road, Plymouth PL6 7PP, United Kingdom

British Library Cataloguing in Publication Information Available

Library of Congress Cataloging-in-Publication Data

Library of Congress Control Number: 2014947273

♾™ The paper used in this publication meets the minimum
requirements of American National Standard for Information
Sciences—Permanence of Paper for Printed Library Materials,
ANSI/NISO Z39.48-1992.

Printed in the United States of America

Contents

(Continued on next page)

Preface

THE COMMON CORE IN GRADES K–3 is the second in a series of comprehensive tools to tap into the vast flow of recently published books for children and teens, offering recommendations of exemplary titles for use in the classroom. Currency meets authority, brought to you by the editors of the highly regarded review sources *School Library Journal* and *The Horn Book Magazine*.

This guide includes hundreds of selections for grades K–3 published since 2007 recommended by *The Horn Book Magazine*. The titles are grouped by subject and complemented by *School Library Journal's* "Focus On" columns, which spotlight specific topics across the curriculum. Providing context for the guide, and suggestions on how to use these resources within a standards framework, is an introduction by Common Core experts Mary Ann Cappiello and Myra Zarnowski. These educators provide perspective on the key changes brought by the new standards, including suggestions on designing lessons and two sample plans.

Following the introduction, you'll find a wealth of books, by category. (Note that the guide is Dewey-Decimal based, so you may want to dig around, for example, in "Social Sciences" to find some titles that you might first seek in "History" or "Science.") Each section includes a listing of the top titles with brief, explicit annotations, and key bibliographic data. "Focus On" articles are appended to appropriate categories to support in-depth curricular development. Each of these articles includes a topic overview and list of current and retrospective resources (including some fiction) and multimedia, enabling educators to respond to the Common Core State Standards call to work across formats.

We hope you find this guide useful, and we welcome any feedback.

— *The Editors*

Introduction

Nonfiction from the Start

Implementing the Common Core State Standards in the Primary Grades (K-3)

Mary Ann Cappiello, Ed.D., *Lesley University*
Myra Zarnowski, Ed.D., *Queens College, CUNY*

SCHOOL CURRICULUM today is in a state of flux. Teachers and school librarians are in the process of asking and answering three persistent questions: What to teach? How to teach it? With what materials? The Common Core State Standards (CCSS), the major force behind current curriculum changes, requires significant shifts in what is happening in schools. But since the CCSS were introduced in 2010, what at first appeared to be an overwhelming list of new demands has become downright familiar. Here are some of these requirements for the primary grades:

Introduce more nonfiction.
Promote reading and reading aloud for key ideas and details.
Examine texts for craft and structure.
Support students' efforts to integrate information.
Have students read and write a variety of text types.
Promote research to build knowledge.

The promotion of more nonfiction reading is key to the CCSS, and it's a good idea to begin introducing it in the primary grades. Why? One of the most convincing reasons is that young children like nonfiction and they can understand it. It's not a hard sell. But there's more. By reading nonfiction, students build background knowledge that is critical for further learning in science, math, social studies, and the arts. Beginning in the primary grades, nonfiction literature can be a gateway to learning content and process in all subject areas.

These curriculum shifts require us to rethink and revise how and what we teach. Quite simply, we need thought provoking, imaginative, and well-written resources, with high quality, relevant illustrative material. We need to locate material for read alouds, guided-reading groups, independent reading, writing workshop, and whole- and small-group instruction.

Fortunately, that material is available, and *The Common Core in Grades K–3* will help you locate it. As we work with exceptional nonfiction and think deeply about it, we can also engage in activities that meet CCSS standards. It's that straightforward. We will also have the opportunity to delve deeply into topics and think about social issues. That is where the true pleasure of teaching and learning resides—not in overdoses of test preparation.

School Library Journal and *The Horn Book Magazine* can help us meet the various standards, whether they are CCSS standards or standards in science, social studies, mathematics, or language arts. They have already identified outstanding nonfiction literature that support teaching and learning. *School Library Journal*—the world's largest reviewer of books, multimedia, and technology for children and teens—evaluates books in terms of literary quality, artistic merit, clarity of presentation, and appeal to intended audience. Their reviews and "Focus On" columns build connections between new and existing titles, making them a valuable resource for finding material that offer comparison opportunities on text features or point of view. Each issue of *The Horn Book Magazine* provides insightful reviews of recommended picture books, fiction, folklore, poetry, and nonfiction, highlighting the outstanding text and illustrative features. *The Horn Book Guide's* semi-annual issue reviews over 2,000 titles—virtually every trade book for youth published in the United States over a six-month period. Between 1989-2014 they have published more than 92,000 reviews. Drawing from this outstanding collection of reviews, this guide identifies the best nonfiction books available for kindergarten through grade three, making it easier for us to build a content-rich foundation for teaching and learning.

What Do I Need to Know About Nonfiction Trade Books?

The requirement that elementary students read 50 percent nonfiction/informational text and 50 percent literature is an important component of any curricular transition to the CCSS. While much energy is focused on aligning teaching methodologies and assessments to the CCSS, it is also important for all who work with students, including administrators, teachers, librarians, and paraprofessionals, to have an understanding of the new kinds of nonfiction picture books that have emerged over the past two decades.

The success of any curricular unit is dependent on the quality of the materials used, the level of engagement those materials provide, and carefully designed classroom activities and assignments. Now more than ever, there are books to match students' interests and teaching requirements. What do you need to know about trade books to make appropriate selections for the classroom?

Nonfiction is Highly Visual

Nonfiction books, like so much else in our world, have become highly visual. Gone are the occasional photographs that might punctuate an informational title. Think brightly colored photographs, archival images, and illustrations in every conceivable type of media. Today's picture and chapter books offer students an opportunity to think about content through text and image. Within picture books, the entire format contributes to its meaning, from the cover illustration to the color or pattern of the end pages to the range of illustrations within; consider, for example, Steve Jenkins's signature cut-paper collage artwork, Kadir Nelson's oil paintings, Nic Bishop's color photography, or the mixed-media collage style of Melissa Sweet. It is important to model for your students how to read the images in a nonfiction book, and to understand the different roles they serve in conveying information and establishing theme. For students in the primary grades, these rich visuals provide even greater points of access and yet another pathway into the content of the text.

Nonfiction for the Primary Grades Offers a Range of Structure and Style

Twenty years ago, primary grade teachers did not have the same range of options for selecting nonfiction for the classroom for children age five to eight. Exemplary titles such as those in the "Let's Read and Find Out" series were few. Today many more nonfiction picture books are published for this age group. The brevity of these books allows for the introduction of sophisticated concepts and ideas, such as food chains or symmetry, in manageable doses. Nonfiction picture books also model a range of writing styles and structures, which you can use to differentiate writing instruction. For those students who prefer to read nonfiction instead of fiction, this increase in options makes it much easier to match books with readers, hook students with a particular book of interest, and encourage children to "stick with it" when the process of learning to read proves difficult.

Because of the range and availability of this material, it's important to note that not all nonfiction picture books for this age group operate as effective read-alouds. Many do, but some don't. It doesn't mean that the book is therefore not a good picture book or useful; it might be a great portal to content information, or a more in-depth read with lots expository rather than narrative text. The more you read, the easier it will be to tell which titles are effective for small-group or individual reading, and which are appropriate to read aloud to an entire class.

Nonfiction Covers a Wide Range of Subjects

In addition to finding abundant picture and chapter books, you'll discover numerous topics covered in today's nonfiction. Within nonfiction, there are subgenres. "If students are unfamiliar with nonfiction texts, they may assume that every nonfiction book serves the same function. This is not the case. Different types of nonfiction books serve varied purposes. Having an understanding of what those purposes are can help students understand why an author selected a particular structure for the book, and how the two work together to create meaning" (Aronson, Cappiello, and Zarnowski, "Deconstructing Nonfiction," January 2013). Subgenres include: survey books, concept books, biography and autobiography, and reference books such as almanacs, atlases, field guides, and how-to titles.

These books employ a variety of structures and styles as well, including narrative, exposition, question and answer, compare and contrast, or problem/solution. Therefore, for any one topic, you might find several books that focus on different subtopics or provide different perspectives.

For example, in this "Go-To Guide," you'll discover a variety of titles that will serve an investigation of coral reefs. Second or third graders can build a foundational knowledge of ocean life by reading Steve Jenkins's *Down, Down, Down: A Journey to the Bottom of the Sea* (HMH, 2009), a concept book about the levels of marine life. Next, students could examine Molly Bang and Penny Chisholm's *Ocean Sunlight: How Tiny Plants Feed the Seas* (Scholastic, 2012) to gain an understanding of photosynthesis and food chains within that environment.

Finally, they could "zoom in" by reading Wendy Pfeffer's *Life in a Coral Reef* (HarperCollins, 2009), comparing and contrasting the information they find there to that in Jason Chin's *Coral Reefs* (Roaring Brook, 2012). Or, students might consider bird communication in general by reading Lita Judge's *Bird Talk* (Roaring Brook, 2012), and then apply that knowledge more specifically to one single bird's extraordinary communicative power when reading Stephanie Spinner's *Alex the Parrot: No Ordinary Bird* (Knopf, 2012), illustrated by Meile So. Alternatively, students could explore the role of specificity in science illustration comparing and contrasting how Steve Jenkins illustrates his own books (for example, *Down, Down, Down* and *The Beetle Book*) to how he illustrates the work of other authors (April Pulley Sayre's *Eat Like a Bear*, Holt, 2013; Pfeffer's *Life in a Coral Reef*). Knowing about the range of books available allows you to incorporate a variety of perspectives and ask students to make the kinds of comparisons they must consider in the CCSS.

Nonfiction Introduces Visible Authors

Nonfiction authors often speak directly to their readers about researching, writing, and interpreting factual information. Their notes are a wonderful source of information to share, offering children insight into how writers sift and shape information, and question the facts they uncover. Introducing primary grade students to an author's process becomes an invaluable framework for their learning, something they can draw from when they read and write. Each of the books below, for example, includes an endnote in which the author discusses his or her work with the readers. These notes highlight different aspects of reading and writing nonfiction for primary grade readers:

> *We March*, written and illustrated by **Shane Evans** (Roaring Brook, 2012). In this brief nonfiction picture storybook, Evans narrates the story of the August 28, 1963 March on Washington for Jobs and Freedom. But unlike most books about this day, Evans's narrative starts quietly, softly, in the early morning hours, as people arise and head towards the buses that will take them to Washington. The arc of the story mirrors the arc of the day and ends with a spread, depicting Martin Luther King's raised arm crossing the pages, and the words "to our dreams." The author's note provides additional background information for readers, discussing the people who spoke at the event, the other marches that took place, the Civil Rights Act of 1964, and the National Voting Rights

Act of 1965. The last two paragraphs of the note move into a personal reflection on the Civil Rights Movement, and the declaration that Evans has "always been inspired by the idea of people coming together." This informative section not only extends the information learned from the text, but gives readers a reflection of the author-illustrator's stance towards the subject matter.

Bird Talk: What Birds are Saying and Why (Roaring Brook, 2012), written and illustrated **Lita Judge**, is an engaging title focusing on bird communication in all its manifestations, from dances to greetings. At the end of the book is a four-page glossary of the animals mentioned, complete with an illustration and short informative text about each creature's habitat, and range, and a few interesting characteristics. A glossary and a list of references and websites follow. Finally, there is Judge's author's note, which includes a photo of her as a girl, with a bird perched on her shoulder. The author reflects on the summers she spent with her grandparents who were ornithologists, and her personal and lifelong connection to these animals. Like Evans, this author/illustrator provided additional information, but more of it. Moreover, her personal experiences are in-depth and focused on her childhood, establishing a connection with young readers.

No Monkeys, No Chocolate, written by **Melissa Stewart** and illustrated by Nicole Wong (Charlesbridge, 2013). In this reverse cumulative picture book, Stewart introduces readers to the rainforest habitat and the interconnection and interdependence of a range of flora and fauna, ultimately concluding with the pivotal role that monkeys play in splitting open cocoa pods and scattering seeds, ensuring another crop. A page on "Cocoa and Rain Forests" is appended, providing readers with an understanding of the differences between traditional cocoa farms and the forest-grown cocoa, while information on "What You Can Do to Help" offers advice on how to advocate for the rainforests, conserve energy, and protect the planet and its animals. Stewart concludes with an "Author's Note" that provides the "backstory" of *Monkeys* and the 10-year period in which she researched, wrote, and rewrote the book. Finally, on her website, is more information about the history of her revisions, including a timeline for the book and shared drafts. By reading *Monkeys*, and the drafts at its different stages, readers gets a fuller sense of Stewart's process and what she strived to do with this particular book.

As you can see, nonfiction trade books are essential sources for learning about content and process. The variety of available formats and features provides many opportunities for teaching and learning across the curriculum. In addition to author's notes, accessing an author's website or interviews with the person provides additional information about the process of writing nonfiction.

Nonfiction Across the Curriculum in Grades K-3: What to Teach? How?

The CCSS did not come with a teacher's guide detailing the content to cover, activities for children, or materials to introduce; it outlined the end goals and challenged us with the task of figuring out how to get there. This has left many educators feeling uncertain about what to do. We love the freedom to construct curriculum, act as decision-makers, and do what we were taught to do—teach creatively with passion and voice. However, we see that the job of implementing CCSS has been placed squarely on our shoulders. It's a big job. But it's a job worth doing.

Creating curriculum involves putting a number of pieces together to make a coherent whole. These pieces consist of the following:

Standards: Content standards such as the Next Generation Science Standards tell us what to teach, while CCSS standards identify the literacy skills to emphasize.

Materials: High quality material helps us get the job done by providing the substance for students to think about.

Hands-On/Minds-On Activities: These are stimulating experiences for students that involve thinking about the topic being studied while learning content and skills.

An Inquiry Stance: Dealing with big questions that don't have simple answers can help keep students focused and remind them that there are always more avenues to explore.

We have found that once we identify a topic, relevant standards, materials, and activities, our lessons fit together in a satisfying way. It all clicks! Putting all the pieces together is challenging, but it also allows us to be creative. It is a rewarding job because it allows librarians and educators to make important decisions about teaching and learning. The following is a sample of how this works in language arts and science.

Language Arts

Students in the primary grades love read alouds. But the read aloud in the primary grades is also a vital instructional practice that allows teachers to introduce content knowledge, model language use, present themes, explore genre, and focus student thinking. Nonfiction read alouds are a wonderful way to model writer's craft. Through them and whole-group conversations, teachers can highlight the writing decisions made by authors, and ask students to explore what the writing "does" in a context that is developmentally appropriate. When given the opportunity to engage in a focused comparison and contrast over several texts, students can begin to understand a writer's craft more deeply.

For example, third graders could explore the use of repetition as a means of highlighting an important point or concept.

> **Standards:** The English-Language Arts Standards for Grade 3 for Reading Informational Text (CCSS.ELA-Literacy.RI.3.8) ask students to: "Describe the logical connection between particular sentences and paragraphs in a text (e.g., comparison, cause/effect, first/second/third in a sequence)." While this standard could be used to support students' understanding of how information is articulated in a work, it can be harnessed to engage in an exploration of the aesthetics of nonfiction writing. Students have been taught to expect nonfiction to be dry and dull; as the books in this guide demonstrate, they are anything but.

> **Nonfiction.** Titles that employ repetition to reinforce concepts include: George Ella Lyon's *All the Water in the World* (S. & S., 2011); Joyce Sidman's *Swirl by Swirl* (HMH, 2011); and April Pulley Sayre's *Turtle, Turtle, Watch Out* (Charlesbridge, 2010).

> **Hands-On/Minds-On Activities.** Read aloud each of the above books, one per day over three days. Start with *All the Water in the World*, the simplest of the group. Ask students to identify what role repetition has in the

book. What words repeat? Where? When? Why? Record this information on a chart with three columns. The next day, read aloud *Turtle, Turtle, Watch Out*. Repeat the process and document student answers on a chart. Finally, read *Swirl by Swirl*, repeating the process for a third time. After reading these books on different science-related topics, query your students about what they have learned about using repetition in writing. How did the repetition help them understand what the book is about? Why did the author choose specific words to repeat? Have students write short informational books on science topics of their choosing, incorporating a strategic use of repetition as a writing device.

Social Studies

Nonfiction provides a foundation of content for social studies inquiries. In the example below, books about the environmental activist Wangari Maathai (1940-2011) explain and illustrate the meaning of active citizenship. Maathai was instrumental in helping the people of Kenya restore the ecological balance of their environment through community tree planting. The selection below will also allow students to consider how individual authors choose to approach a topic.

Standards: The College, Career, and Civic Life (C3) Framework for Social Studies Standards emphasize the role of civics in the primary-grade curriculum (D2.Civ.6.K-2). According to these standards, by the end of grade two, students should be able to "describe how communities work together to accomplish tasks, establish responsibilities, and fulfill roles of authority."

Nonfiction: Use the following nonfiction titles to build background about how Maathai worked with her community to plant trees: Jen Cullerton Johnson and Sonia Lynn Sadler's *Seeds of Change* (Lee and Low, 2010); Claire Nivola's *Planting the Trees of Kenya* (FSG, 2008); and Jeanette Winter's *Wangari's Trees of Peace* (HMH, 2008).

Hands-On/Minds-On Activities. After reading aloud *Wangari's Trees of Peace*, *Planting the Trees of Kenya*, and *Seeds of Change*, work with students to complete the chart below to gather information about conditions in Maathai's village. What was life in her village like before she left for the

United States? What was it like when she returned? What was it like after the women of her village made changes?

Conditions in Kenya

Before Maathai Left Kenya	When Maathai Returned to Kenya	After Maathai worked with women

Using the completed chart, have students write an explanation of how the people in Maathai's village were able to make changes that benefitted everyone. Ask students to use evidence from the books to support their ideas.

As you can see from these two examples—one in language arts and one in social studies—by combining standards, nonfiction literature, and hands-on/minds-on activities, we can create the curriculum we need.

Becoming Decision-Makers

The standards' documents provide us with goals to meet, but not the route. It's up to us to become decision makers, deciding how to teach and what materials to use. We have the opportunity to be creative while responding to students' interests and to select materials and design lessons around them. *The Common Core in Grades K–3* will be a valuable tool as we shape the curriculum in our classrooms and libraries.

As you and your team continue to realign your curriculum to the CCSS and consider new ways to explore language arts, science, social studies, and the arts, this guide is something you can turn to again and again to learn about exemplary nonfiction texts. The following questions might also help you navigate the guide:

—What is the content of the curriculum standards I must teach in this particular unit?

—What subheading should I go to first to find the trade books that match the content?

—What are the subgenres of nonfiction that provide a range of approaches to the topic?

—How does the book review point me toward ways that I can use this book in the classroom for content and language arts curriculum?

Using the "Go-To Guide" to select trade books for your curriculum puts you in the driver's seat. It's not necessary to purchase an expensive program to meet the Common Core State Standards. By gathering the resources that you already have to create new curriculum units, and/or working with your school librarian to purchase text sets of books to revise existing lesson plans, you can construct engaging curriculum that will be meaningful for your students. This is the best way we know to accept the challenge of creating curriculum.

* * * * *

Arts

🜚 **Bryant, Jen.** A Splash of Red: The Life and Art of Horace Pippin. 40 pp. Knopf (Random House Children's Books) 2013. ISBN 978-0-375-86712-5. LE ISBN 978-0-375-96712-2. Illustrated by Melissa Sweet. series.

Horace Pippin created dozens of paintings, based on memories from his childhood and experiences in World War I, stories his grandmother told, stories from the Bible, and scenes he saw around him. Bryant's well-researched, articulate account of Pippin's life is interspersed with direct quotes from him, most of which are embedded directly into Sweet's expressive gouache, watercolor, and collage illustrations. Reading list, websites.

Visual Arts; African Americans; Painting; Artists; Biographies; Pippin, Horace

◯ **Cline-Ransome, Lesa.** Benny Goodman & Teddy Wilson: Taking the Stage as the First Black-and-White Jazz Band in History. 32 pp. Holiday 2014. ISBN 978-0-8234-2362-0. Illustrated by James E. Ransome.

Goodman grew up in Chicago, a working-class Jewish boy; Wilson lived in Tuskegee, Alabama, a middle-class African American boy. The story of how the two jazz musicians met and formed the Benny Goodman Trio (the "first interracial band to perform publicly") is recounted in short bursts of text, almost like jazz riffs, accompanied by pencil and watercolor illustrations that capture distinctive moments. Timeline.

Individual Biographies; Wilson, Teddy; Goodman, Benny; Bands; Musicians; Music—Jazz; Race relations; Jews; African Americans

E
E **Ehlert, Lois.** The Scraps Book: Notes from a Colorful Life. 72 pp. Simon/Beach Lane 2014. ISBN 978-1-4424-3571-1.

In a generously illustrated picture book memoir, Ehlert speaks directly to her audience, particularly readers who like collecting objects and making things. The book is jam-packed with her art and photos from her life: her parents, the house she grew up in, and the small table where she was encouraged to pursue her art; along the way, we see how autobiographical her books have been.

Visual Arts; Artists; Illustrators; Autobiographies; Women—Autobiographies; Women—Artists; Biographies; Women—Biographies

Gonyea, Mark. A Book About Color: A Clear and Simple Guide for Young Artists. 96 pp. Holt 2010. ISBN 978-0-8050-9055-0.

Gonyea's square format, generous use of space, and breezy, informal style work well with the topic. We learn about warm and cool colors, the emotional impact of colors, and the color wheel. Individual chapters and a text that covers only one simple idea per spread allow concepts to sink in. The casual tone makes new terminology and ideas seem less daunting.
Visual Arts; Color

Greenberg, Jan and Jordan, Sandra. Ballet for Martha: Making Appalachian Spring. 48 pp. Roaring Brook/Flash Point/Porter 2010. ISBN 978-1-59643-338-0. llustrated by Brian Floca.

After choreographer Martha Graham asked composer Aaron Copland and sculptor/set designer Isamu Noguchi to collaborate with her on a new ballet, the iconic *Appalachian Spring* was born. Using spare, concise sentences, the authors echo Graham's approach to dance: nothing's wasted, and in such exactness lies beauty. Floca's fluid, energetic line and watercolor illustrations also reflect the plain boldness of Graham's choreography. Websites. Bib.
Performing Arts; Dance—Ballet; Composers; Choreographers; Graham, Martha; Women—Biographies; Biographies; Women—Choreographers; Noguchi, Isamu; Copland, Aaron; Artists

Isadora, Rachel. There Was a Tree. 32 pp. Penguin/Paulsen (Penguin Young Readers Group) 2012. ISBN 978-0-399-25741-4.

Isadora recasts "The Green Grass Grew All Around," setting it in Africa. As the verses accumulate, the subject of each line is shown as a rebus; complete lyrics and musical notation are included. Bright blue birds star in the collage illustrations, standing out dramatically against the earth-tone foregrounds and stark white backgrounds. A fine contribution to picture books based on children's songs.
Music; Animals—Savanna animals; Rebuses; Cumulative tales; Africa; Songs; Trees

Markel, Michelle. The Fantastic Jungles of Henri Rousseau. 40 pp. Eerdmans 2012. ISBN 978-0-8028-5364-6. Illustrated by Amanda Hall. series.

Markel's informative text conveys self-taught modern artist Henri Rousseau's ground breaking flat perspective, inspiration by faraway lands, and determined personality,

as well as interesting details such as his place in a circle of Modernist artists and writers. Hall's lush watercolor and acrylic art bears a clear resemblance to Rousseau's. This successful tribute makes Rousseau accessible, and inspirational, to a young audience.

Visual Arts; Rousseau, Henri; Painting; Artists; Biographies; France; Jungles; Creativity

Parker, Marjorie Blain. Colorful Dreamer: The Story of Artist Henri Matisse. 32 pp. Dial 2012. ISBN 978-0-8037-3758-7. Illustrated by Holly Berry.

This picture-book biography opens in a dreary French village where the young Henri Matisse didn't "excel at much of anything—except, perhaps, dreaming." As the story describes his years as an artist, Berry's illustrations directly mimic Matisse's Fauvist use of color and maturing style. Parker's lyrical text and Berry's impressive mixed-media pictures fully encompass Matisse's chronology, aspirations, and talents.

Visual Arts; Artists; Painting; Biographies; France; Matisse, Henri; Dreams and dreaming

Rosenstock, Barb. The Noisy Paint Box: The Colors and Sounds of Kandinsky's Abstract Art. 40 pp. Knopf (Random House Children's Books) 2014. ISBN 978-0-307-97848-6. LE ISBN 978-0-307-97849-3. Illustrated by Mary GrandPré.

Pioneering abstract artist Vasily Kandinsky experienced "colors as sounds, and sounds as colors," a neurological condition called synesthesia. Concentrating primarily on Kandinsky's childhood, Rosenstock embellishes known events with dialogue. GrandPré does a fine job showing color and sound as abstractions while presenting the artist and his surroundings realistically. An author's note provides more information about the artist and four reproductions. Websites. Bib.

Visual Arts; Biographies; Sound; Color; Painting; Artists; Synesthesia; Russia (Federation); Kandinsky, Wassily

Stringer, Lauren. When Stravinsky Met Nijinsky: Two Artists, Their Ballet, and One Extraordinary Riot. 32 pp. Harcourt (Harcourt Trade Publishers) 2013. ISBN 978-0-547-90725-3.

Although Stringer overplays the degree of collaboration between composer and choreographer, there's no doubt that they created something beautifully, brutally new in *The Rite of Spring* in 1913 Paris. Acrylic illustrations dance right along in a sweep of movement and color that owes as much to Matisse as to their own lively

spirit. Notes about the ballet and Stringer's visual inspirations are appended. Bib.
Performing Arts; Composers; Choreographers; Stravinsky, Igor; Dance—Ballet; Paris (France); Nijinsky, Vaslav

Tate, Don. It Jes' Happened: When Bill Traylor Started to Draw. 32 pp. Lee 2012. ISBN 978-1-60060-260-3. Illustrated by R. Gregory Christie.

This picture-book biography describes artist Traylor's life—born into slavery in 1854, he worked as a sharecropper after Emancipation—and how at the age of eighty-five he first began to draw on scraps of cardboard. Christie's own flat primitive style is a perfect match for Traylor's story, but the real artistry here is in Tate's finely crafted account of Traylor's first eighty years.
Visual Arts; Folk art; Alabama; Traylor, Bill; Biographies; Artists; African Americans

Winter, Jeanette. Henri's Scissors. 40 pp. Simon/Beach Lane 2013. ISBN 978-1-4424-6484-1.

Winter focuses on Henri Matisse's later life, during which the painter took up collage and discovered the magic he could make with scissors. Winter's text is straightforward and unflowery, and she includes quotes from the artist regarding this revelation. Winter relies, successfully, on the strength of her own art to capture the essence of Matisse's; cut paper is integrated into the illustrations.
Visual Arts; Artists; Matisse, Henri; Collage; Painting

Winter, Jonah. Just Behave, Pablo Picasso! 48 pp. Scholastic/Levine 2012. ISBN 978-0-545-13291-6. Illustrated by Kevin Hawkes.

Winter's energetic account focuses on the painter's unquenchable inventiveness, tracing his rise from prodigy through several controversial styles and from the furor over his African mask–inspired *Les Demoiselles d'Avignon* to his revolutionary cubist *Girl with a Mandolin*. With his broad brush strokes and painterly art, Hawkes evokes Picasso's oeuvre without imitating it, an impressive achievement. A concluding note provides context but no sources.
Visual Arts; Biographies; Picasso, Pablo; Artists; Painting

● ●

—FOCUS ON—
Musicians & Fine Artists

Brushes with Greatness

By Wendy Lukehart

*Wendy Lukehart is the Youth Collections Coordinator
at the District of Columbia Public Library.*

● ●

Many baby boomers loved the inspiring narratives of the "orange biographies" ("Childhood of Famous Americans" Series) as children but those who became librarians were later influenced by professional standards to rail against invented dialogue and fictional scenarios in their workplace collections. How delightful that the burgeoning format of the last two decades—picture book biographies—presents a satisfying solution to this dilemma. Although we expect our informational picture books to be fact-based, to have a bibliography (and possibly citations), to contain back matter and some sense in the author's note where liberties were taken, this is a format through which freedom rings. It is the role of the creator(s) to imagine the parts of a life not known and to add to the truth of the interpretation through photographs, reproductions of art, realia, or original illustrations.

The work of visual artists is particularly suited to this format, and because children are innately drawn in by intriguing images, these books are pathways to any time period. Authors and illustrators have to work harder to convey the core of a musician's life, because the melody, harmony, timbre, rhythm, and the rest of the musical vocabulary are missing. The word choices, size and placement of fonts, style and mood of the art, and other visual elements must convey the essence of how, for example, the music of Handel and Hendrix differs. In addition to being captivating introductions to a diverse range of talented individuals, these titles offer avenues to address the Common Core State Standards, whether students "… describe the relationship between illustrations and the text…" (RI.K.7), "Compare and contrast the overall structure…of events, ideas, concepts, or information in two or more texts" (RI.5.5), or undertake myriad other critical thinking skills.

MUSICIANS

Anderson, M. T. Handel, Who Knew What He Liked. illus. by Kevin Hawkes. Candlewick. 2001. Tr $14.99. ISBN 9780763665999; pap. $4.99. ISBN 9780763666002.

Gr 1-6–A wry, tongue-in-cheek narrative highlights Handel's naughty, self-indulgent, flamboyant persona from childhood on, while simultaneously showcasing his genius. Enhancing the child appeal with more funny business, Hawkes's acrylics also conjure the beauty of snowfall in Hamburg or the moonlit *Water Music* performed on the Thames. Insets define musical terms.

Capaldi, Gina & Q. L. Pearce, adapts. Red Bird Sings: The Story of Zitkala-Ša, Native American Author, Musician, and Activist. illus. by Gina Capaldi. Carolrhoda. 2011. Tr $17.95. ISBN 9780761352570.

Gr 2-6–Paraphrased from semiautobiographical articles, this longer-than-average picture book text depicts an extraordinary Sioux life, from childhood in a tipi to a violin performance for a president (1900). Zitkala-Ša applied musical, journalistic, and advocacy talents toward advancing Indian rights. Mixed-media compositions include newspaper clippings and her opera score.

Chambers, Veronica. Celia Cruz, Queen of Salsa. illus. by Julie Maren. Dial. 2005. RTE $15.99. ISBN 9780803729704; pap. $6.99. ISBN 9780142407790.

K-Gr 3–Acrylic and collage depictions of Cuba's songbird employ a sizzling palette and snippets of music to show Cruz's childhood, career with a popular band, and momentous decision to leave home for a Hollywood club. Pair with Monica Brown's *Tito Puente: Mambo King/Rey del mambo* (Rayo, 2013), a bilingual biography of the drummer, bandleader, and frequent collaborator. Audio version available from Recorded Books.

Cline-Ransome, Lesa. Before There Was Mozart: The Story of Joseph Boulogne, Chevalier de Saint-George. illus. by James E. Ransome. Random/Schwartz & Wade. 2011. Tr $17.99. ISBN 9780375836008; lib. ed. $20.99. ISBN 9780375936210.

Gr 1-5–The dramatic use of light and shadow heightens this fascinating account of the mixed-race son of a West Indies plantation owner and his slave. Boulogne was afforded a privileged status that led to education, violin lessons, residency in Paris, and a musical career rivaling his contemporary, Mozart.

○ **Golio, Gary.** Jimi: Sounds Like a Rainbow: A Story of the Young Jimi Hendrix. illus. by Javaka Steptoe. Clarion. 2010. Tr $16.99. ISBN 9780618852796.
Gr 2-8–"Could someone paint pictures with sound?" From his imitation of the "plink" of rain with a childhood ukulele to later experimentation with guitar and amplifier, Hendrix's life and innovations are orchestrated around this question. Reclaimed wood, psychedelic background collages, and contrasting ghost figures capture the electricity of a rock star.

○ **Golio, Gary.** When Bob Met Woody: The Story of the Young Bob Dylan. illus. by Marc Burckhardt. Little, Brown. 2011. Tr $17.99. ISBN 9780316112994.
Gr 1-4–Acrylic and oil panoramas of the Midwest and portraits of musical inspirations such as Hank Williams and Odetta surround a youthful Bob Zimmerman. Trains, miners, and strikes dominate his landscape, until he falls under Woody Guthrie's spell. Singing by his folk hero's hospital bed transforms the young man's fledgling career.

○ **K'naan & Sol Guy.** When I Get Older: The Story Behind "Wavin' Flag." illus. by Rudy Gutierrez. Tundra. 2012. Tr $17.99. ISBN 9781770493025.
Gr 1-5–This first-person account describes rapper/songwriter K'naan's childhood in war-torn Somalia and adolescence as a refugee in Toronto. His grandfather's poetry, particularly the piece alluded to in the title (which became a world anthem during the 2010 World Cup), gave him strength. Art combining photorealism and surreal distortion adds emotional depth.

○ **Parker, Robert Andrew.** Piano Starts Here: The Young Art Tatum. illus. by author. Random/Schwartz & Wade. 2008. Tr $17.99. ISBN 9780375839658; ebk. $10.99. ISBN 9780307983558.
K-Gr 4–Warm colors present cameos of the legendary jazz pianist's parents and reveal their support as he struggles with failing vision but succeeds at the piano. Writing in the first-person and ultimately moving to cool, impressionistic scenes, Parker builds a world experienced through smells, sounds, and feelings. Evocative and effective.

J
92

Pinkney, Andrea Davis with Scat Cat Monroe. Ella Fitzgerald: The Tale of a Vocal Virtuosa. illus. by Brian Pinkney. Hyperion/Jump at the Sun. 2002. Tr $16.99. ISBN 9780786805686.

K-Gr 5–Feisty narrator Scat Cat takes the swing and bebop queen from Yonkers to Carnegie Hall. The high-octane text is alliterative and sassy, driven by internal rhymes, similes, rhythm, and period vocabulary. Pulsating scratchboard scenes show the performer swinging in a battle of the bands and flying with Dizzy Gillespie. Audio version available from Recorded Books.

Ryan, Pam Muñoz. When Marian Sang: The True Recital of Marian Anderson. illus. by Brian Selznick. Scholastic. 2002. Tr $17.99. ISBN 9780439269674.

K-Gr 5–Anderson's journey, beginning in a church choir, blocked at Constitution Hall, and culminating at the Metropolitan Opera, is presented as performance and symbolic triumph. Spirituals punctuate Ryan's heartfelt and historically accurate text, soaring with meaning when layered with Selznick's coppery acrylics of Anderson, eyes closed, her faith deeply felt in song.

Shefelman, Janice. I, Vivaldi. illus. by Tom Shefelman. Eerdmans. 2008. Tr $18. ISBN 9780802853189.

K-Gr 5–Fact and fiction (distinguished in an endnote) combine to pit a mother's vow during childbirth (that her son will become a priest) against his adolescent wish—becoming a musician. Against a painterly backdrop of Venetian canals, cathedrals, and palaces, the ordained violinist ultimately conducts an orchestra of orphans playing heavenly compositions.

Sís, Peter. Play, Mozart, Play! illus. by author. HarperCollins/Greenwillow. 2006. Tr $16.99. ISBN 9780061121814; lib. ed. $17.89. ISBN 9780061121821.

K-Gr 5–Whimsical ink and watercolor compositions contextualize the child prodigy's "play" (practicing and performing)–and his lack of play (frivolity with other children). Clever designs imagine his exterior and interior worlds. Pair with Elizabeth Rusch's *For the Love of Music* (Tricycle, 2011) to compare Wolfgang to his talented sister, Maria Anna.

Stanbridge, Joanne. The Extraordinary Music of Mr. Ives: The True Story of a Famous American Composer. illus. by author. Houghton Mifflin. 2012. RTE $16.99. ISBN 9780547238661.

Gr 1-5–Stanbridge juxtaposes watercolor and ink renderings of the 1915 *Lusitania* with the unconventional musical ideas flowing to an American composer working in Manhattan, with all its cacophony. Following the disastrous news, Ives and fellow commuters find comfort in a hurdy-gurdy's hymn. That melody mingles with street sounds in the resulting composition, "From Hanover Square North."

○ **Stringer, Lauren.** When Stravinsky Met Nijinsky: Two Artists, Their Ballet, and One Extraordinary Riot. illus. by author. Houghton Harcourt. 2013. RTE $16.99. ISBN 9780547907253.
K-Gr 3–An alliterative and onomatopoeic text intersects with the colors and styles of contemporaries Matisse and Picasso for a book that is musically and visually sensitive to its subjects. From the humorous-sounding title to the notion that a ballet (*The Rite of Spring*) could provoke fistfights—this entertains as it informs.

○ **Winter, Jonah.** The Fabulous Feud of Gilbert & Sullivan. illus. by Richard Egielski. Scholastic/Arthur A. Levine. 2009. Tr $16.99. ISBN 978 0439930505.
Gr 1-4–Opera leaps to life in this factually based narrative. Arguments, a miniature stage, wooden dolls, kimonos, swords, and silly names ("Titipu" and "Yum-Yum") invite interest in the Victorian librettist's and composer's relationship and work, specifically *The Mikado*. Watercolor and ink characters promenade in the foreground against ever-changing scenery.

VISUAL ARTISTS

○ **Aston, Dianna Hutts.** Dream Something Big: The Story of the Watts Towers. illus. by Susan L. Roth. Dial. 2011. RTE $17.99. ISBN 9780803732452.
PreS-Gr 3–Italian immigrant Simon Rodia's single-handed construction of 100-foot towers and a boat in Los Angeles is described in blank verse through the eyes of a (fictional) young neighbor. Mixed-media mosaics portray him stirring cement, bending iron rods, and pressing "a jigsaw of jewels" (shells, mirrors, tiles) into today's national landmark. Photographs included.

○ **Bryant, Jen.** A Splash of Red: The Life and Art of Horace Pippin. illus. by Melissa Sweet. Knopf. 2013. Tr $17.99. ISBN 9780375867125l; lib. ed. $20.99. ISBN 9780375967122.
Gr 1-4–Childlike, mixed-media collages are the perfect medium to chronicle the self-taught, African American painter's lifelong interest in creating art, despite a paucity of supplies and, later, a crippling war injury. Quotes are presented graphically, adding to the inspirational effect of his progress and eventual success. Pippin's works appear on the endpapers.

J
92 **Fritz, Jean.** Leonardo's Horse. illus. by Hudson Talbott. Putnam. 2001. Tr $21.99. ISBN 9788811580478.
Gr 2-6–The book's curved top carves the vaulted ceilings of Renaissance Florence and the 1990s Pennsylvania dome under which the plans for da Vinci's 24-foot bronze horse were finally realized. The first half profiles the multifaceted artist;

the second shows the lengths to which an art collector went to make a 15th-century dream come true.

J
92
Pollock

Greenberg, Jan & Sandra Jordan. Action Jackson. illus. by Robert Andrew Parker. Roaring Brook. 2002. Tr $16.95. ISBN 9780761316824; lib. ed. $22.90. ISBN 9780761327707; pap. $7.99. ISBN 9780312367510.
Gr 1-4–Research informs this account of Jackson Pollock's process and motivation as he conceived his famous drip painting *Number 1, 1950 (Lavender Mist)*—reproduced at the climax. Loose, dappled watercolors imagine the enormous canvas spread across the floor and the moment the artist "begins his dance." Meticulous notes expand the text.

○ **Harvey, Jeanne Walker.** My Hands Sing the Blues: Romare Bearden's Childhood Journey. illus. by Elizabeth Zunon. Marshall Cavendish. 2011. Tr $17.99. ISBN 978 0761458104; ebk. $9.99. ISBN 9780761460633.
PreS-Gr 3–Told in the rhyme scheme and three-line structure of a blues song, this narrative shows the artist reflecting on his childhood move from Charlotte to Harlem during the Great Migration. An authentic work featuring his favorite motifs—trains, chickens, North Carolina, guitars—is incorporated into Zunon's oil and mixed-media collages. Audio version available from Recorded Books.

○ **Leach, Deba Foxley.** Grant Wood: The Artist in the Hayloft. (Adventures in Art Series). Prestel. 2005. Tr $14.95. ISBN 9783791334011.
Gr 1-6–The cover image of rolling hills, stylized trees, and a farmhouse is indicative of Wood's regional style. Numerous reproductions are arranged in a dynamic design, while short paragraphs with well-chosen information and questions engage and guide readers in closer inspection. This title exemplifies the strengths of an outstanding series.

○ **Novesky, Amy.** Georgia in Hawaii: When Georgia O'Keeffe Painted What She Pleased. illus. by Yuyi Morales. Houghton Harcourt. 2012. RTE $16.99. ISBN 9780152054205.
K-Gr 4–O'Keeffe makes a deal with the Hawaiian Pineapple Company in 1939: three months on the islands for two paintings of pineapples. Heated disagreements arise and are ultimately resolved. Lush acrylic and digital compositions of flowers, water, and landforms, rendered in brilliant fuchsias and greens, are inspired by the artist's style and subjects.

Penrose, Antony. The Boy Who Bit Picasso. photos by Lee Miller. Abrams. 2011. Tr $16.95. ISBN 9780810997288.

K-Gr 5–Readers are treated to a fresh view of Picasso—as family friend; the male narrator's mother was a photographer. Through her marvelous images, readers see the home, studio, and art of a fun-loving man who provided masks for guests, kept a goat outside his bedroom, and liked to roughhouse. Delightful.

J
92
Stanley, Diane. Michelangelo. illus. by author. HarperCollins. 2000. Tr $15.95. ISBN 9780688150853; pap. $6.99. ISBN 9780060521134.

Gr 3-7–With a longer text than usual for a picture-book biography, this title offers lucid social and historical commentary about a Renaissance man, from birth through death. Through clever digital manipulation, Stanley's paintings portray Michelangelo at work on the *Pietà, David, Sistine Chapel,* and other famous pieces. Processes, from dissecting cadavers to designing frescoes, are explored.

E
S
Stone, Tanya Lee. Sandy's Circus: A Story About Alexander Calder. illus. by Boris Kulikov. Viking. 2008. RTE $16.99. ISBN 9780670062683.

K-Gr 4–While Stone's focus is the creation of and performances surrounding the mechanical circus crafted from wire, fabric, cork, and found objects, the author shows how Calder's upbringing encouraged such play and how his skills, education, and experience ultimately led to the invention of mobiles. Mixed-media collages emphasize big hands manipulating delicate wonders.

Winter, Jonah. Frida. illus. by Ana Juan. Scholastic/Arthur A. Levine. 2002. Tr $17.99. ISBN 9780590203203.

PreS-Gr 3–Fanciful, folkloric creatures—a cuddly skeleton, jaguar, and devil—accompany this Mexican girl who escapes the pain of polio and a bus accident through drawing and painting. Juan's magical realm conveys the spirit of Kahlo's art. Pair this with Duncan Tonatiuh's *Diego Rivera: His World and Ours* (Abrams, 2011) to learn about her husband.

Wolf, Gita. Following My Paint Brush. illus. by Dulari Devi. Tara Books. 2010. Tr $18.50. ISBN 9789380340111.

PreS-Gr 3–Simple, first-person sentences narrate Devi's life in an impoverished Indian village and the impact of discovering art. Her employment as a "cleaner woman" for an artist and the consequent tutelage led to transformation. Intricate patterns dominated by small black lines and flat colors depict people, animals, and domestic life.

Young, Ed. The House Baba Built: An Artist's Childhood in China. illus. by author. Little Brown. 2011. Tr $17.99. ISBN 9780316076289.

Gr 3-8–Cricket battles, rooftop roller-skating, and silkworms contrast with bombs, fighter planes, and food rationing in Young's account of childhood in China during the 1930s and '40s. Postcards, maps, magazine images, family photographs, and acrylic portraits make each page turn a surprise, while gatefolds extend the scale of Baba's (Young's father) expansive fortress.

DIGITAL PICKS

For Students

Alexander Calder's Circus (Part 1). www.youtube.com/watch?v=iT_qA_WI47U. The Anthony Roland Collection of Films on Art. Société Nouvelle Pathé Cinéma. (Accessed 6/19/14).

Gr 1-6–This nine-minute excerpt presents Calder performing with his miniature circus in Paris. The artist sets up a ring and uses ingenious mechanical devices to manipulate a belly dancer, sword thrower, lion tamer, and acrobat who flips onto a running horse, and other amazing spectacles. A marvelous blend of art and engineering.

Marian Anderson: A Life in Song. www.library.upenn.edu/exhibits/rbm/anderson. Curated by Nancy M. Shawcross. University of Pennsylvania. (Accessed 6/19/14).

Gr 3 Up–Building on a 1994 exhibition, this site breaks Anderson's life into logical segments. Each has several informative paragraphs and revelatory photographs, musical scores, programs, recordings, and video clips, including the performance at the Lincoln Memorial. Comprehensive and accessible.

Tito Puente–"Mambo Birdland." video.nationalgeographic.com/video/music/genre-wm /salsa/mambo-birdland-wm. National Geographic. (Accessed 6/19/14).

K Up This five-minute segment features close-ups of the high-energy Latino drummer playing percussion for a mambo in a 1950s New York ballroom. The camera pans the room, capturing the precision of the brass musicians and the fancy footwork and costumes of the dancers. A video of Celia Cruz is available on the same page.

For Teachers

Classical Kids Music Education. www.classicalkidsnfp.org. (Accessed 6/20/14).

Long respected for introducing children to composers' lives and music through their fact-based, award-winning CDs and DVDs, such as *Vivaldi's Ring of Mystery*, this organization now offers a touring repertoire (complete with actors, costumes, musical scores, props, and sets) to perform these stories with local orchestras. Educator resources relate to the media and concerts.

Smithsonian American Art Museum. americanart.si.edu/education/resources. Smithsonian Institution. (Accessed 6/20/14).
From "African American Artists" to "Latino Voices in American Art," this site presents a wealth of resources for educators who wish to introduce art across content areas. Topics are explored through images and interpretation, biography, video interviews with artists, and top-notch lesson plans. The target audience is K-12.

MoMA Learning. http://www.moma.org/learn/moma_learning. Museum of Modern Art. (Accessed 6/19/14).
Customizable and downloadable resources, including slideshows, work sheets, and video clips featuring curators and museum educators discussing MoMA's collections, offer myriad possibilities for classroom instruction in modern and contemporary art education. Search by theme or artist, or browse through movements such as Abstract Expressionism and Dada.

MEDIA PICKS

By Phyllis Mandell

Listen to the Birds: An Introduction to Classical Music. CD. 26 min. with book. The Secret Mountain. 2013. ISBN 9781923163895. $16.95.
K-Gr 2–The London Symphony Orchestra, The Radio Symphony Orchestra of Moscow, and the Toronto Chamber Orchestra are among the groups that perform excerpts of 20 classical pieces, all of which represent the voices of birds. Music from *Peter and the Wolf, The Carnival of Animals, Swan Lake,* and *The Magic Flute* is all part of the melodic mix. The accompanying book includes notes about the composers, a glossary of musical terms, and a time line.

My Hands Sing the Blues: Romare Bearden's Childhood Journey. By Jeanne Walker Harvey. Cassette or CD. 15 min. Recorded Books. 2012. Cassette ISBN 9781464002090, CD ISBN 9781464002069. $15.75; hardcover book ISBN 9780761458104. $17.99.
K-Gr 3–Narrator Kevin R. Free reads Harvey's lyrical account of the artist's life and gives the rhyming lines the cadence of a blues song. This stirring blend of words and images is a perfect introduction to Bearden, the Great Migration, and the Harlem Renaissance.

Blues in All Flavors. CD. 42 min. with booklet. Prod. by Hot Toddy Music. Dist. by NewSound Kids. 2012. ISBN unavail. $14.98.

PreS-Gr 4–Singer Gaye Adegbalola presents a variety of original songs about childhood concerns delivered with a bluesy flavor. Her themes include getting outside and dancing, interpersonal relationships, and the importance of kindness, and the selections include jump blues with boogie-woogie, doo-wop, Chicago blues with stop time, and reggae rhythm.

---

*Eds. Note: The full version of "Brushes with Greatness"
is available online at http://ow.ly/ye9iK.*

Biography

J
92

Asim, Jabari. Fifty Cents and a Dream: Young Booker T. Washington. 48 pp. Little 2012. ISBN 978-0-316-08657-8. Illustrated by Bryan Collier. series.

The emphasis of this brief portrait of Booker T. Washington is on his quest for knowledge: as a young boy living in slavery, wanting to learn to read, and then as a young adult attending the Hampton Institute. Watercolor and collage illustrations show the powerful determination on the subject's face, and everything about the bookmaking reverberates with the importance of books and learning. Timeline. Bib.

Individual Biographies; Washington, Booker T.; African Americans; Teachers; Education

J
92

Berne, Jennifer. On a Beam of Light: A Story of Albert Einstein. 48 pp. Chronicle 2013. ISBN 978-0-8118-7235-5. Illustrated by Vladimir Radunsky

Berne and Radunsky—in a gorgeous piece of bookmaking—use the "biggest, most exciting thought Albert had ever had" as the focal point for their homage to the great physicist. Berne's simple text shows the adult Albert's child-friendly inclinations (ice-cream walks, an aversion to socks), while Radunsky's spontaneous line work creates a sense of movement that perfectly mirrors Albert's endless search for answers.

Individual Biographies; Physics; Einstein, Albert; Scientists; Nobel Prize

Bober, Natalie S. Papa Is a Poet : A Story About Robert Frost. 40 pp. Holt 2013. ISBN 978-0-8050-9407-7. Illustrated by Rebecca Gibbon.

The author of *A Restless Spirit* draws on that fuller biography for a picture book focused on the pivotal years (1900–12) when Frost lived in Derry, New Hampshire. Skillfully, Bober introduces Frost's idiosyncrasies along with his gifts and frequently incorporates lines from Frost's poems. Gibbon's acrylic, pencil, and watercolor art captures the era's essence. A fine introduction to Frost.
Frost, Robert; Poets

Brown, Don. A Wizard from the Start: The Incredible Boyhood and Amazing Inventions of Thomas Edison. 32 pp. Houghton (Houghton Mifflin Trade and Reference Division) 2010. ISBN 978-0-547-19487-5.

Young Thomas Edison worked hard, mixed chemicals, cultivated curiosity, and read a lot of books. These are the seeds of the inventor's success as presented by Brown in this unfussy picture book biography, illustrated with softly glowing watercolors. Readers will appreciate Brown's depiction of an "incredible boyhood," which here means finding one's passions at a young age and pursuing them with gusto. Bib.
Individual Biographies; Edison, Thomas A.; Inventions and inventors

Brown, Monica. Pablo Neruda: Poet of the People. 32 pp. Holt 2011. ISBN 978-0-8050-9198-4. Illustrated by Julie Paschkis.

Brown opens with Neftali's boyhood love of reading, writing, and nature, celebrating the subjects that informed his poetry and his "dreams of peace." Paschkis's signature effusions of color and stylized forms are embellished with words—in English, Spanish, and other languages—poetically related in both sound and sense. It all adds up to an intriguing dramatization of Neruda's themes and concerns. Reading list, websites.
Individual Biographies; Neruda, Pablo; Poets; Chile; Poetry; Nobel Prize

Brown, Monica. Tito Puente: Mambo King / Rey del mambo. 32 pp. HarperCollins/Rayo 2013. ISBN 978-0-06-122783-7. Illustrated by Rafael López.

A bilingual picture book charts the life of Tito Puente with all the exuberance of the drummer and bandleader's irresistible music. Vibrant imagery hums right off the page, full of high-contrast color and energetic composition, and decorated with swirling, starry embellishments. The treatment is not especially deep and is decidedly positive: Tito's life reads like a sequence of successes.

Individual Biographies; Foreign languages—Spanish language; Music—Latin music; Puente, Tito; Musicians; Harlem (New York, NY); Hispanic Americans

Burleigh, Robert. Night Flight: Amelia Earhart Crosses the Atlantic. 40 pp. Simon/Wiseman 2011. ISBN 978-1-4169-6733-0. Illustrated by Wendell Minor.

Burleigh's vivid free-verse account of Earhart's 1932 flight from Newfoundland to Northern Ireland, the first-ever solo transatlantic flight by a woman, settles into the cockpit and describes what the legendary pilot might have seen and felt during that long, tense, exhilarating trip. Minor's paintings heighten the immediacy, depicting Earhart's blazing red Vega in both long shots and close-ups. Websites. Bib.

Individual Biographies; Flight; Pilots; Women—Pilots; Women—Biographies; Vehicles—Airplanes; Earhart, Amelia

Christensen, Bonnie. I, Galileo. 40 pp. Knopf (Random House Children's Books) 2012. ISBN 978-0-375-86753-8. LE ISBN 978-0-375-96753-5.

More straightforward if less individual than Peter Sis's *Starry Messenger*, this is an excellent introduction to the scientist. The illustrations not only give geographical and historical context for Galileo's ideas and experiments but also convey the arc of the narrative. Diagrams illustrating some of Galileo's key concepts are clear and executed in a harmonious style. Bib., glos., ind.

Individual Biographies; Scientists; Physics; Italy; Astronomy; Galileo

Cline-Ransome, Lesa. Before There Was Mozart: The Story of Joseph Boulogne, Chevalier de Saint-George. 40 pp. Random/Schwartz & Wade 2011. ISBN 978-0-375-83600-8. LE ISBN 978-0-375-93621-0. Illustrated by James E. Ransome.

Cline-Ransome gives a lively account of the great "mulatto" violinist. The text describes both what a man of his parentage could and couldn't do in eighteenth-century France and also his accomplishments. Ransome's lustrous mixed-media paintings illumine Boulogne's tropical Guadeloupe birthplace and distinguished Parisian venues with equal panache; he gives his subject an appealing intensity and intelligence that ripen into quiet authority.

Individual Biographies; Music—Classical music; Mixed-race people; Musicians; Composers; Blacks; Saint-Georges, Joseph Boulogne, Chevalier de; Musical instruments—Violin; France

E
C

Codell, Esmé Raji. Seed by Seed: The Legend and Legacy of John "Appleseed" Chapman. 32 pp. Greenwillow (HarperCollins Children's Books Group) 2012. ISBN 978-0-06-145515-5. LE ISBN 978-0-06-145516-2. Illustrated by Lynne Rae Perkins. series.

Two contemporary urban children meet colonial-era orchardist John "Appleseed" Chapman and accompany him around the country as he communes with nature and shares its bounty. Codell's lyrical text paints a heroic portrait; Perkins's detailed, homespun watercolor and gouache illustrations embrace the natural world, evoking its sounds, smells, and changing seasons. An author's note includes craft ideas and an apple pie recipe.

Individual Biographies; Chapman, John; Appleseed, Johnny; Fruits and vegetables—Apples; History, American—Frontier and pioneer life; Nature

O

Cummins, Julie. Flying Solo: How Ruth Elder Soared into America's Heart. 32 pp. Roaring Brook 2013. ISBN 978-1-59643-509-4. Illustrated by Malene R. Laugesen.

In 1927, inspired by Charles Lindbergh, Elder took off in the *American Girl* for Paris. When the plane crashed into the Atlantic, Elder (after her dramatic rescue) became a celebrity. The second half of Cummins's picture book biography recounts Elder's airplane racing adventures. The text captures the feel of the era while pastel illustrations capture the lofty feeling of flying. Reading list, websites.

Individual Biographies; Women—Biographies; Vehicles—Airplanes; Pilots; Women—Pilots; Elder, Ruth

O

Ferris, Jeri Chase. Noah Webster & His Words. 32 pp. Houghton (Houghton Mifflin Trade and Reference Division) 2012. ISBN 978-0-547-39055-0. Illustrated by Vincent X. Kirsch.

In this unique biography of the patriot and dictionary writer, Ferris seamlessly incorporates words with their definitions—"He wanted to write a DIC-TION-AR-Y (noun: a book listing words in ABC order, telling what they mean and how to spell them)"—creating opportunities for vocabulary development, but also showing what Webster's work was all about. Kirsch's humorous illustrations highlight important moments. Timeline, websites. Bib.

Individual Biographies; Teachers; Dictionaries; Language—Vocabulary; Webster, Noah; History, American—Revolutionary War; Books and reading

○ **Glaser, Linda.** Emma's Poem: The Voice of the Statue of Liberty. 32 pp. Houghton (Houghton Mifflin Trade and Reference Division) 2010. ISBN 978-0-547-17184-5. Illustrated by Claire A. Nivola.

Glaser's account of how Emma Lazarus came to write her iconic poem is brief, yet telling—especially when complemented by Nivola's eloquent illustrations. Her rectilinear compositions and poses; generalized figures; and bright, limited palette capture New York City's opulent upper crust and the indigent yet dignified newcomers with equal skill. An author's note and the text of the poem are appended.

Individual Biographies; Women—Poets; Poets; Women—Biographies; Statue of Liberty (New York, NY); Statues; Lazarus, Emma; Women—Jews; Jews

E
H **Heiligman, Deborah.** The Boy Who Loved Math: The Improbable Life of Paul Erdös. 40 pp. Roaring Brook 2013. ISBN 978-1-59643-307-6. Illustrated by LeUyen Pham.

Heiligman presents the nomadic mathematician Paul Erdös as an appealing eccentric: for instance, Paul referred to children as "epsilons" ("a very small amount in math"). Each of Pham's illustrations is a puzzle for the reader to solve, with complex numerical concepts integrated into the pictures. While the overall layout is high in appeal, the font size is too small for the target audience.

Individual Biographies; Mathematics; Erdös, Paul

E
H **Hopkins, H. Joseph.** The Tree Lady: The True Story of How One Tree-Loving Woman Changed a City Forever. 32 pp. Simon/Beach Lane 2013. ISBN 978-1-4424-1402-0. Illustrated by Jill McElmurry.

Kate Sessions, the first woman to graduate from Berkeley with a science degree, was responsible for populating San Diego's Balboa Park with lush, green trees, just in time for the Panama-California Exposition in 1915. Hopkins's text succinctly captures the highlights of his subject's life, and McElmurry's gouache illustrations document the gradually changing landscape from barren desert to verdant garden.

Individual Biographies; Women—Biographies; San Diego (CA); Trees; Sessions, Kate

J
92 **Hopkinson, Deborah.** Annie and Helen. 40 pp. Random/Schwartz & Wade 2012. ISBN 978-0-375-85706-5. LE ISBN 978-0-375-95706-2. Illustrated by Raul Colón. series.

This book looks at challenges Helen Keller and teacher Annie Sullivan faced and surmounted. Annie's point of view is considered as much as Helen's, and Annie's strength of character is highlighted. Peppered with excerpts from Annie's letters, the book concludes with the first letter Helen writes on her own. Colón's line and watercolor pictures are rather sedate; endpapers provide photographs. Reading list, websites.

Individual Biographies; Keller, Helen; Sullivan, Annie; Disabilities, Physical—Deafness; Disabilities, Physical—Blindness; Letters; Women—Biographies; Women—Teachers; Teachers

Jones, Carrie. Sarah Emma Edmonds Was a Great Pretender: The True Story of a Civil War Spy. 32 pp. Carolrhoda 2011. ISBN 978-0-7613-5399-7. Illustrated by Mark Oldroyd. Sarah Edmonds, disguised as a man, fought alongside and spied for Union troops during the Civil War. Jones enumerates these feats with touches of humor, and she continues Sarah's story throughout the war and her subsequent marriage. Oldroyd makes effective use of broad, rough-hewn brush strokes, particularly in creating an impressionistic background that frequently allows a detailed illustration of Sarah to take center stage. Bib.

Individual Biographies; Women—Spies; History, American—Civil War; Women—Biographies; Spies; Edmonds, Sarah Emma; Gender roles; Nurses; Women—Nurses; Soldiers

Kalman, Maira. Looking at Lincoln. 40 pp. Penguin/Paulsen (Penguin Young Readers Group) 2012. ISBN 978-0-399-24039-3.
A girl passes a Lincoln look-alike and wonders about our sixteenth president. Through a natural structure that follows the narrator's thought processes, the narrative lists some basic facts; childlike musings, printed in a more casual font, personalize the account. A gloomy funeral scene is depicted in grays and blacks, a sobering note among the profusion of bright, colorful gouache illustrations. Bib.

Individual Biographies; Lincoln, Abraham; Presidents—United States

Kalman, Maira. Thomas Jefferson: Life, Liberty and the Pursuit of Everything. 40 pp. Penguin/Paulsen (Penguin Young Readers Group) 2014. ISBN 978-0-399-24040-9. Kalman's colloquial, occasionally arch, and whimsical narrative is heavy with historical import and dotted with trivia about Jefferson's life at Monticello. A series of spreads, with Kalman's familiar primitivist rendering and chromatic brilliance, details Jefferson's work as collector, architect, horticulturalist, and musician. The vibrant imagery, frank content, and disarming language combine in a nuanced portrait that respects its subject and its audience.

Individual Biographies; Presidents—United States; Jefferson, Thomas; Virginia; Monticello (VA)

Kohuth, Jane. Anne Frank's Chestnut Tree. 48 pp. Random 2013. ISBN 978-0-449-81255-6. LE 978-0-375-97115-0. PB 978-0-307-97579-9. Illustrated by Elizabeth Sayles. Nature, as represented by a chestnut tree outside the Secret Annex, serves as a continuing image for this easy reader. The tree's presence throughout Anne's life in hiding not only gives her a sense of peace but also provides readers a respite from her ordeal. Illustrations are somber except those depicting Anne's pre-war life or Annex visits from helpers bringing food and books. Reading list. Website.

Frank, Anne; Women—Biographies; Jews; Netherlands; History, Modern—Holocaust

J
92

Krull, Kathleen. Jim Henson: The Guy Who Played with Puppets. 40 pp. Random (Random House Children's Books) 2011. ISBN 978-0-375-85721-8. LE ISBN 978-0-375-95721-5. Illustrated by Steve Johnson.

Krull's straightforward text highlights key events and includes anecdotes to round out Henson's motivational life story. Johnson and Fancher's colorful paintings capture the vitality in their subject's life and work. This celebration of Henson and his love of puppetry is a timely way to mark the late artist's seventy-fifth birthday and introduce the man and his puppets to a whole new generation. Bib.

Individual Biographies; Television; Puppets; Henson, Jim

O **Krull, Kathleen and Brewer, Paul.** Lincoln Tells a Joke: How Laughter Saved the President (and the Country). 32 pp. Harcourt (Harcourt Trade Publishers) 2010. ISBN 978-0-15-206639-0. Illustrated by Stacy Innerst.

It's his sense of humor, rather than a single wisecrack, that Krull and Brewer explore through Lincoln's quips. Departing from Lincoln's levity is the inclusion of less amusing, but perhaps more instructive, information on his love of language, grammar, and elocution. Innerst displays his own sense of humor by creating near-caricatures that exaggerate Lincoln's long, lanky frame and numerous bad hair days. Bib.

Individual Biographies; Lincoln, Abraham; Presidents—United States; Jokes

Q **Krull, Kathleen and Brewer, Paul.** The Beatles Were Fab (and They Were Funny). 40 pp. Harcourt (Harcourt Trade Publishers) 2013. ISBN 978-0-547-50991-4. Illustrated by Stacy Innerst.

Krull and Brewer tell the story not just of international superstars but of friends who made one another laugh. Drawn with exaggerated features, the lads are all legs and bowl-cut hair, their ample noses serving to distinguish one from the others. Youngsters wondering why the band is still beloved by their parents and grandparents will understand after reading the humorous anecdotes. Timeline. Bib.

Individual Biographies; Music—Rock music; Bands; Musicians; Beatles; Humorous stories; Friendship

Lawlor, Laurie. Rachel Carson and Her Book That Changed the World. 32 pp. Holiday 2012. ISBN 978-0-8234-2370-5. Illustrated by Laura Beingessner.

From the naturalist's early fascination with wildlife to her determination to finish her landmark work, *Silent Spring*, before her death, this accessible account folds a commendable amount of significant information into picture book format. Beingessner's spacious ink and tempera spreads reflect the upbeat tone and Carson's most passionate concerns. An epilogue describes the watershed effect of *Silent Spring*. Bib.

Individual Biographies; Scientists; Women—Scientists; Authors; Women—Biographies; Biology; Natural history; Environment; Carson, Rachel; Women—Authors

Markel, Michelle. Brave Girl: Clara and the Shirtwaist Makers' Strike of 1909. 32 pp. HarperCollins/Balzer + Bray 2013. ISBN 978-0-06-180442-7.Illustrated by Melissa Sweet. series.

In her simple but powerful text, Markel shows how multiple arrests, physical attacks, and misogyny failed to deter Clara Lemlich as she set off on her lifelong path as a union activist in the early twentieth century. Clara's story is accentuated by Sweet's vivid illustrations, many of which are presented on fabric scraps or torn paper with borders of machine stitching. Bib.

Individual Biographies; Lemlich, Clara; Women—Labor leaders; Labor leaders; Strikes and lockouts; Women—Biographies

McCarthy, Meghan. Daredevil: The Daring Life of Betty Skelton. 48 pp. Simon/Wiseman 2013. ISBN 978-1-4424-2262-9.

In the 1940s, Betty Skelton wanted to become a commercial pilot or to fly in the navy, but those avenues were closed to females, so she went on to aerobatic flying, always accompanied by her dog, Little Tinker. The sometimes choppy prose is balanced by a soaring tale, brought to life in illustrations featuring charming bug-eyed characters and a vivid palette. Timeline. Bib.

Individual Biographies; Skelton, Betty; Pilots; Women—Pilots; Women—Biographies; Sports—Automobile racing

McDonnell, Patrick. Me...Jane. 40 pp. Little 2011. ISBN 978-0-316-04546-9.

McDonnell's inspirational book focuses on the great primatologist's formative years; young Jane, with her stuffed toy chimp, studies nature wherever and however she can.

Homey, earth-toned pen and watercolor pictures, simple and intimate, are accented with casually arrayed stamped motifs and some of Goodall's childhood drawings. A note about Goodall's current projects and "A Message from Jane" are appended.
Individual Biographies; Women—Biographies; Goodall, Jane; Women—Zoologists; Zoology; Animals—Chimpanzees; Scientists; Women—Scientists; Toys

Moss, Marissa. Nurse, Soldier, Spy: The Story of Sarah Edmonds, A Civil War Hero. 48 pp. Abrams 2011. ISBN 978-0-8109-9735-6. Illustrated by John Hendrix.
During the Civil War, Sarah Edmonds, disguised as a man, fought for the Union. Her dedication and bravery also made her the perfect spy. Moss emphasizes Sarah's early work and initial mission, concluding the biography before war's end. Hendrix's art, heavily shaded in orange for battle scenes or somber blue for makeshift field hospitals, emphasizes the horror and drama of war. Bib., glos., ind.
Individual Biographies; Edmonds, Sarah Emma; History, American—Civil War; Women—Biographies; Women—Nurses; Nurses; Women—Spies; Spies; Soldiers; Gender roles

Moss, Marissa. The Bravest Woman in America. 32 pp. Tricycle (Ten Speed Press) 2011. ISBN 978-1-58246-369-8. LE ISBN 978-1-58246-400-8. Illustrated by Andrea U'Ren.
After illness disabled her lighthouse keeper father, Ida Lewis took over his duties. In 1858, at age sixteen, she heroically rescued four boys whose boat had capsized—the first of many rescues during a lifelong career. The stirring events are beautifully visualized in painterly watercolor, ink, and acrylic art. An author's note further highlights the significance of Ida's career.
Individual Biographies; Rhode Island; Lighthouses; Women—Biographies; Emotions—Courage; Vehicles—Boats and boating; Lewis, Ida

Nivola, Claire A. Life in the Ocean: The Story of Oceanographer Sylvia Earle. 32 pp. Farrar/Foster 2012. ISBN 978-0-374-38068-7.
Earle's intimate knowledge of the creatures she's spent over half a century observing, whether while snorkeling near the surface or walking on the ocean floor, permeates this enthusiastic biography illustrated with exquisitely detailed watercolor art. An author's note explains why we all need to get involved in efforts to curtail the threats of overfishing, climate change, oil spills, and other pollutants. Bib.
Individual Biographies; Scientists; Oceanography; Women—Biographies; Women—Explorers; Women—Scientists; Women—Marine biologists; Marine biology; Exploration and explorers; Earle, Sylvia; Environment—Conservation

E
P

Pinborough, Jan. Miss Moore Thought Otherwise: How Anne Carroll Moore Created Libraries for Children. 40 pp. Houghton (Houghton Mifflin Trade and Reference Division) 2013. ISBN 978-0-547-47105-1. Illustrated by Debby Atwell. series.
This easygoing picture-book biography gives us a simple narrative of Anne Carroll Moore's Maine childhood and early love of books on through to her career at the New York Public Library. With sun-dappled acrylic paintings of, first, rural Maine and, later, triumphantly, the light-filled interiors of NYPL's new Children's Room, the tone here is one of uncomplicated optimism, reflecting Moore's practical idealism. Bib.
Individual Biographies; Books and reading; New York (NY); Maine; Women—Librarians; Women—Biographies; Libraries

○ **Provensen, Alice.** The Buck Stops Here: The Presidents of the United States. 64 pp. Viking 2010. ISBN 978-0-670-01252-7. New ed., 1990, Harper.
This twentieth-anniversary edition of Provensen's overview of U.S. presidents (updated through President Obama) depicts each man surrounded by symbols, placards, headlines, and other materials that illustrate his administration. The drawings have a primitive, cluttered charm. The short verses are sometimes funny and sometimes acute character sketches. Appended notes expand the text. First class for browsing. Bib.
Collective Biographies; Presidents—United States

○ **Rappaport, Doreen.** Helen's Big World: The Life of Helen Keller. 40 pp. Hyperion 2012. ISBN 978-0-7868-0890-8. Illustrated by Matt Tavares. series.
Rappaport covers the span of Helen's life from birth through her years with Annie Sullivan and after. The focus is on Helen, but readers get an acute awareness of Annie's sacrifices for her. Tavares's illustrations (ink, watercolor, and gouache) are bold and often in close-up, while quotes heighten the emotion of this stirring and awe-inspiring book. Reading list, timeline, websites. Bib.
Individual Biographies; Keller, Helen; Sullivan, Annie; Disabilities, Physical—Deafness; Disabilities, Physical—Blindness; Women—Biographies

○ **Rappaport, Doreen.** Jack's Path of Courage: The Life of John F. Kennedy. 48 pp. Hyperion 2010. ISBN 978-1-4231-2272-2. Illustrated by Matt Tavares.
A smiling Jack Kennedy greets readers on the jacket of Rappaport's latest picture book biography. Following a familiar pattern, she intersperses quotes from her subject with basic biographical information, here stressing Kennedy's bravery and devotion to duty. In Tavares's varied watercolor and pencil illustrations, a soft pal-

ette depicts idyllic settings while more dramatic incidents are shown in bright, bold colors. Reading list, timeline. Bib.

Individual Biographies; Presidents—United States; Kennedy, John F.

Rusch, Elizabeth. Electrical Wizard : How Nikola Tesla Lit Up the World. 40 pp. Candlewick 2013. ISBN 978-0-7636-5855-7. Illustrated by Oliver Dominguez.  The only biography about Tesla published for young readers introduces an individual who knows what he wants to accomplish (an alternating current generator) but struggles to turn that idea into a tangible product. Stylized illustrations surround Tesla with scientific instruments while utility poles and wires crowd the New York City streets. The book's back matter is particularly strong. Reading list. Bib.

Tesla, Nikola; Electricity; Scientists

Rusch, Elizabeth. For the Love of Music: The Remarkable Story of Maria Anna Mozart. 32 pp. Tricycle (Ten Speed Press) 2011. ISBN 978-1-58246-326-1. LE ISBN 978-1-58246-391-9. Illustrated by Steve Johnson.

There was another Mozart prodigy: "At twelve, Maria was considered one of the best pianists in Europe." Not only did she tour with her soon-to-be-renowned little brother, she was his inspiration and playfellow. Rusch's text, echoing sonata form, is appropriately bittersweet. A two-page "encore" adds more about Maria. The illustrators evoke eighteenth-century Salzburg in collages of brocades overlaid with painted detail and musical notation. Bib.

Individual Biographies; Women—Biographies; Mozart, Maria Anna; Musicians; Musical instruments—Piano; Women—Musicians

Schmidt, Gary D. Martín de Porres: The Rose in the Desert. 32 pp. Clarion 2012. ISBN 978-0-547-61218-8. Illustrated by David Diaz. series.

Martín de Porres (1579–1639), a beloved Peruvian Dominican monk, was canonized in 1962 as the patron saint of universal brotherhood. Schmidt's graceful account of his life focuses mostly on Martín's impoverished youth among Lima's slaves and Indians. Diaz's visualization of this story is magnificent: rich in Latin American hues, the mixed-media art extends the text on each lovely spread.

Individual Biographies; de Porres, Martín; Peru; Mixed-race people; Religion—Christianity; Religion—Saints; Poverty; Religion—Monks

J
9 2.

Schroeder, Alan. Ben Franklin: His Wit and Wisdom from A-Z. 32 pp. Holiday 2011. ISBN 978-0-8234-1950-0. Illustrated by John O'Brien.
In this alphabetical compendium of Franklin highlights, each spread features a letter or two initializing significant places, inventions, people, and more. Details are dramatized in deftly ordered boxes, banners, and balloons; all are rendered in O'Brien's old-timey pen and ink and brightened with watercolor. The bits of narrative text are usefully straightforward, and aphorisms recognizable as Poor Richard's are sprinkled throughout.
Individual Biographies; Franklin, Benjamin; Concept books—Alphabet books; History, American—Colonial life; Inventions and inventors; Statesmen; Scientists

O **Schubert, Leda.** Monsieur Marceau. 40 pp. Roaring Brook/Porter 2012. ISBN 978-1-59643-529-2. Illustrated by Gérard DuBois. series.
In this biography of Marcel Marceau (alter-ego, mime Bip), declarative sentences artfully capture the performer's essence. The emphasis is on Marceau as an artist, but Schubert doesn't shy away from his persecution as a Jew during the Holocaust. DuBois's vigorous illustrations strikingly cast Marceau as a mostly white figure against black backgrounds. An afterword and miming tips are appended. Reading list.
Individual Biographies; Performing arts; Jews; History, Modern—Holocaust; France; Marceau, Marcel; Mimes

O **Skrypuch, Marsha Forchuk.** One Step at a Time: A Vietnamese Child Finds Her Way. 104 pp. Pajama Press 2013. ISBN 978-1-927485-01-9. PE ISBN 978-1-927485-02-6.
This sequel to *Last Airlift* describes Tuyet's adjustment to life with her adoptive Canadian family, the drama this time revolving around the surgery she must have on her leg due to polio. Readers will be just as riveted to this quieter but no-less-moving story as Tuyet bravely dreams of being able to run and play. Illustrated with photos. Reading list, websites. Ind.
Individual Biographies; Disabilities, Physical; Vietnam; Adoption; Orphans; Surgery; Diseases—Polio; Immigration; Canada; Son Thi Anh, Tuyet

O **Spielman, Gloria.** Marcel Marceau: Master of Mime. 32 pp. Kar-Ben 2011. ISBN 978-0-7613-3961-8. PE ISBN 978-0-7613-3962-5. Illustrated by Manon Gauthier.
Spielman's understated picture book biography covers fascinating events of Marceau's early life. At sixteen, he and his brother fled the Nazis and became active in the French Resistance. Because of his ability to entertain, Marcel was tapped to smuggle Jewish children out of France. Gauthier's softly colored line drawings per-

fectly capture the gentle spirit of the performer, both off and on stage.

Individual Biographies; Performing arts; France; Marceau, Marcel; Jews; History, Modern—Holocaust; History, Modern—World War II

E
S

Stone, Tanya Lee. Who Says Women Can't Be Doctors?: The Story of Elizabeth Blackwell. 40 pp. Holt/Ottaviano 2013. ISBN 978-0-8050-9048-2. Illustrated by Marjorie Priceman. Doctor Elizabeth Blackwell's early life is outlined in trim conversational prose in this lively picture-book treatment. A choice handful of biographical elements are arranged artfully to develop Blackwell's character within the expectations and challenges of her time. Priceman's gouache illustrations lend a perfect framework of energy and pacing to the text and draw upon its provocative and often humorous tone. Bib.

Individual Biographies; Women—Biographies; Medicine; Women—Doctors; Gender roles; Doctors; Blackwell, Elizabeth

E
S

Sweet, Melissa. Balloons over Broadway: The True Story of the Puppeteer of Macy's Parade. 40 pp. Houghton (Houghton Mifflin Trade and Reference Division) 2011. ISBN 978-0-547-19945-0.

Marionette maker Tony Sarg designed mechanical storybook figures for Macy's window displays before inventing the giant balloon characters that would become the signature feature of the Macy's Thanksgiving Day Parade. Sweet's whimsical mixed-media collages, embellished with little dolls she made herself out of odds and ends, reinforce the theme that, for Sarg, work was play. An author's note and source list are appended. Bib.

Individual Biographies; Puppets; Parades; Sarg, Tony; Holidays—Thanksgiving; New York (NY); Stores; Hot-air balloons

J
92

Van Allsburg, Chris. Queen of the Falls. 40 pp. Houghton (Houghton Mifflin Trade and Reference Division) 2011. ISBN 978-0-547-31581-2.

At the turn of the twentieth century, Annie Edson Taylor, widowed and elderly, decides she'll go over Niagara Falls in a barrel, a feat never before attempted. Though the stunt seems miraculous, Van Allsburg's matter-of-fact narrative emphasizes her advance technical planning. Sepia-toned illustrations depict Annie as prim and proper but also convey her grit and determination. An author's note is appended. Bib.

Individual Biographies; Waterfalls; Women—Biographies; Niagara Falls (NY and Ont.); Taylor, Annie Edson; Gender roles

Winter, Jeanette. The Watcher: Jane Goodall's Life with the Chimps. 48 pp. Random/Schwartz & Wade 2011. ISBN 978-0-375-86774-3. LE ISBN 978-0-375-96774-0.

In this tranquil picture book biography, the theme of persistence shapes spare, inviting text, which takes Goodall from backyard observations to scientific study of chimpanzees in Tanzania. Winter's signature stylized paintings show the jungle in cool blues and greens. Overall the volume gives an accurate, visually appealing account of Goodall's discoveries and her transition from watching chimpanzees to campaigning to save them.
Individual Biographies; Women—Biographies; Women—Zoologists; Zoology; Goodall, Jane; Scientists; Women—Scientists; Animals—Chimpanzees

Folktales & Nursery Rhymes

Aesop. Mouse & Lion. 32 pp. Scholastic/di Capua 2011. ISBN 978-0-545-10147-9. Illustrated by Nancy Ekholm Burkert.

Nancy Ekholm Burkert brings her meticulous style to Aesop's classic, setting it—as did Jerry Pinkney in *The Lion and the Mouse*—in Africa. Rand Burkert's character-revealing, story-advancing dialogue is the sort to captivate a group. It's an admirable complement to the matchless Pinkney volume, sure to invite productive comparison. Author's and illustrator's notes are appended.
Folktales/Myths/and Legends; Fables; Animals—Lions; Animals—Mice; Folklore—Animals; Africa

Ahlberg, Allan. The Goldilocks Variations. 32 pp. Candlewick 2012. ISBN 978-0-7636-6268-4. Illustrated by Jessica Ahlberg. series.

With six tongue-in-cheek variants, the Ahlbergs (father and daughter) progress from simple changes in the canonical tale's details and repartee to a version with thirty-three bears. The verbal wit, the delicately limned pen and watercolor art with its plenitude of intriguing detail, and clever touches of paper engineering add up to a barrel of fun. Re-reading will ensue.
Folktales/Myths/and Legends; Toy and movable books; Animals—Bears; Humorous stories

◖ **Alley, Zoë B.** There's a Princess in the Palace. 40 pp. Roaring Brook/Porter 2010. ISBN 978-1-59643-471-4. Illustrated by R. W. Alley.

The Alleys create an impressive royal lineage that links *Cinderella, Sleeping Beauty, Snow White*, etc. As in *There's a Wolf at the Door,* this oversized book begs groups of children to gather round, finding amusing details in the smartly rendered comic-book panels and sharing the puns and jokes; a pair of mice play Rosencrantz and Guildenstern, offering wisecracks throughout.

Folktales/Myths/and Legends; Humorous stories; Cartoons and comics; Princes and princesses

◖ **Bryan, Ashley.** Can't Scare Me! 40 pp. Atheneum (Simon & Schuster Children's Publishing) 2013. ISBN 978-1-4424-7657-8.

In this sprightly rhymed retelling, a little boy who "knew no fear" scoffs at his

grandma's warnings about a two-headed giant. But then he's captured by an even fiercer three-headed giant. The boy uses his wits—and musical ability—to escape with a new understanding of the difference between bravery and daring. Rainbow-colored tempera and watercolor illustrations effectively portray a truly scary giant.

Folktales/Myths/and Legends; Folklore—Africa; Blacks; Family—Grandmothers; Monsters; Emotions—Fear; Stories in rhyme

◖ **Daly, Jude.** Sivu's Six Wishes: A Taoist Tale. 32 pp. Eerdmans 2010. ISBN 978-0-8028-5369-1.

The Stone Cutter is translated here to a contemporary setting, one guesses South Africa. Stonemason Sivu wishes he could be a wealthy businessman—then becomes that man. Sivu next becomes the mayor, the sun, a cloud, etc., each time misusing his power. Daly's art, in a rich, clear palette, is quietly stunning, revealing the beauty both in harsh landscapes and mundane streetscapes.

Folktales/Myths/and Legends; Wishes; Religion—Taoism; Africa

◖ **DeFelice, Cynthia.** Nelly May Has Her Say. 32 pp. Farrar/Ferguson 2013. ISBN 978-0-374-39899-6. K-3 Illustrated by Henry Cole. series.

When red-haired Nelly May heads up the hill in search of employment with Lord Pinkwinkle, the requirements of the job are to memorize his eccentric names for things: water is "rivertrickle," boots are "stompinwhackers," etc. DeFelice and

Cole do a fine job of amending an absurdist English folktale; Cole's illustrations don't try to be too clever, and forefronted action makes it perfect for storytime.
Folktales/Myths/and Legends; Humorous stories; Work; Folklore—England

Divakaruni, Chitra Banerjee. Grandma and the Great Gourd: A Bengali Folktale. 32 pp. Roaring Brook/Porter 2013. ISBN 978-1-59643-378-6. Illustrated by Susy Pilgrim Waters. Along the way to her daughter's house, Grandma talks three animals out of eating her by convincing them to wait for her return trip. Divakaruni's retelling of a Bengali folktale evokes the oral tradition by frequent use of pattern and onomatopoeia. Waters's mixed-media collages are perhaps too pretty, but they give a sense of depth through layering and textures.
Folktales/Myths/and Legends; Family—Grandmothers; Folklore—India; Jungles

Galdone, Paul. The Gingerbread Boy. 48 pp. Houghton (Houghton Mifflin Trade and Reference Division) 2011. ISBN 978-0-547-59940-3. Folk Tale Classic series. New ed., 1975, Seabury.

——. The Three Billy Goats Gruff. 48 pp. Houghton (Houghton Mifflin Trade and Reference Division) 2011. ISBN 978-0-547-57655-8. Folk Tale Classic series. New ed., 1973, Seabury.

These two books from the 1970s appear in a uniform paper-over-board edition. Galdone was a refreshingly modest illustrator: his retellings are straightforward and his unassumingly loose-lined, color-separated pictures provide just enough embellishment. Plenty of white space gives the stories all the room they need.
Folktales/Myths/and Legends

Galdone, Paul. The Little Red Hen. 48 pp. Houghton (Houghton Mifflin Trade and Reference Division) 2011. ISBN 978-0-547-37018-7.Folk Tale Classic series. New ed., 1973, Seabury.

——. The Three Bears. 40 pp. Houghton (Houghton Mifflin Trade and Reference Division) 2011. ISBN 978-0-547-37019-4. Folk Tale Classic series. New ed., 1972, Seabury.

——. Three Little Kittens. 40 pp. Houghton (Houghton Mifflin Trade and Reference Division) 2011. ISBN 978-0-547-57575-9. Folk Tale Classic series. New ed., 1986, Clarion.

——. The Three Little Pigs. 48 pp. Houghton (Houghton Mifflin Trade and Reference Division) 2011. ISBN 978-0-547-37020-0. Folk Tale Classic series. New ed., 1970, Seabury.

These four books appear in a uniform paper-over-board edition. Galdone was a refreshingly modest illustrator: his retellings are straightforward and his unassumingly loose-lined, color-separated pictures provide just enough embellishment, as when the lazy cat in *The Little Red Hen* lolls on the couch, dreaming of sardines.
Folktales/Myths/and Legends; Animals—Hens; Behavior—Laziness; Folklore—Animals

Grimm, Jacob and Grimm, Wilhelm. The Frog Prince or Iron Henry. 32 pp. North-South 2013. ISBN 978-0-7358-4140-6. Illustrated by Binette Schroeder. Reissue, 1989.
A warm, uncluttered rendering of the familiar tale of the distressed princess and an enchanted frog. The spare rendering of text and pictures, shot through with understated humor, holds broad appeal for personal reading and story hour use.
Folktales/Myths/and Legends; Animals—Frogs; Princes and princesses; Books in translation; Folklore—Germany

Harrington, Janice N. Busy-Busy Little Chick. 32 pp. Farrar 2013. ISBN 978-0-374-34746-8. Illustrated by Brian Pinkney.
In this story from the Nkundo people of Central Africa, Mama Nsoso's chicks are shivering in their nest at night. She promises they'll build a new "ilombe" (house), but, instead, each day something yummy begs to be eaten. "Busy-busy" Little Chick gets to work, gathering materials and building. Harrington uses repetitive elements and refrains to keep children participating, while Pinkney creates energetic watercolors.
Folktales/Myths/and Legends; Behavior—Perseverance; Animal homes; Animals—Chickens; Folklore—Africa

Karas, G. Brian. Young Zeus. 48 pp. Scholastic 2010. ISBN 978-0-439-72806-5.
In simple, colloquial language ("'Who are you?'...'I'm your mother,' said Rhea. 'Give me a hug.' But...'You missed all my birthdays!' said Zeus'"), Karas renders myth into farce, with cartoonlike characters ranging from the appealing boy god to his monstrous dad. Amusing (if at times a bit scary), this is a singularly irreverent take on an ancient creation story.
Folktales/Myths/and Legends; Zeus (Greek deity); Mythology, Greek; Gods and goddesses; Greece, Ancient

Kimmel, Eric A. The Spider's Gift: A Ukrainian Christmas Story. 32 pp. Holiday 2010. ISBN 978-0-8234-1743-8. Illustrated by Katya Krenina.
When her mother discovers spiders living in the family's Christmas tree, Katrusya insists the tree remain indoors to keep the creatures from freezing. The spiders

reward Katrusya's kindness by turning their webs to silver. Kimmel incorporates Ukrainian words and phrases into the text for better appreciation of the folktale and culture. Krenina's oil paintings, in lush, warm tones, are quietly festive.
Folktales/Myths/and Legends; Animals—Spiders; Holidays—Christmas; Folklore—Ukraine; Folklore—Animals

○ **Lee, H. Chuku.** Beauty and the Beast. 32 pp. HarperCollins/Amistad 2014. ISBN 978-0-688-14819-5. Illustrated by Pat Cummings.
Giving Cummings's lushly detailed paintings center stage, Lee simplifies the tale and puts it into Beauty's first-person voice. While the retelling retains the story's original details, the pictures portray all of the characters as black, in settings inspired by West Africa. The retelling is crisp, the drafting is skillful, and the compositions are dramatic. Princess-lovers of any color should enjoy it.
Folktales/Myths/and Legends; Folklore—France; Princes and princesses

○ **Lunge-Larsen, Lise.** The Troll with No Heart in His Body and Other Tales of Trolls from Norway. 96 pp. Minnesota 2013. ISBN 978-0-8166-8457-1. New ed. Illustrated by Betsy Bowen.
This new edition of native Norwegian Lunge-Larsen's collection (still available from Houghton as an ebook) contains nine tales (plus a brief bonus story). The author's satisfying retellings and additional commentary about trolls honor the spirit of their oral origins. Bowen's rustic woodcuts, with their earthy colors, thick lines, and enormous, ugly trolls, pay homage to traditional Norwegian woodcarving and design.
Trolls; Folklore—Norway

○ **MacDonald, Margaret Read.** The Boy from the Dragon Palace. 32 pp. Whitman 2011. ISBN 978-0-8075-7513-0. Illustrated by Sachiko Yoshikawa.
A poor flower-seller receives a gift from the Dragon King: a boy "who had the snottiest nose you ever did see!" After being fed, the boy blows his nose and gold covers the floor. The man then makes demand after demand. Bright, digitally enhanced watercolor collage sets the story in Japan, with traditional clothing contrasting nicely with the funny details.
Folktales/Myths/and Legends; Folklore—Japan; Humorous stories; Luck; Behavior—Greed

J
398.209 **Manna, Anthony L. and Mitakidou, Soula.** The Orphan: A Cinderella Story from Greece. 40 pp. Random/Schwartz & Wade 2011. ISBN 978-0-375-86691-3. LE ISBN 978-0-375-96691-0. Illustrated by Giselle Potter.

Melding and modernizing a couple of traditional versions, Manna and Mitakidou fashion a lyrical *Cinderella* variant. The girl known here as "the orphan" seeks help at her mother's grave. Mother Nature and her children bring the girl gifts, including "delicate blue shoes." Potter grounds the action with figures whose faces convey universal emotions, their expressive body language arrayed on minimal, richly hued backgrounds.

Folktales/Myths/and Legends; Cinderella stories; Folklore—Greece; Orphans; Princes and princesses

○ **Mathers, Petra.** The McElderry Book of Mother Goose: Revered and Rare Rhymes. 96 pp. McElderry (Simon & Schuster Children's Publishing) 2012. ISBN 978-0-689-85605-1. series.

Drawn mostly from the canonical Opies, Mathers's fifty-seven entries include many lesser-known or longer rhymes, all nicely leavened with such familiar nonsense as "Hey Diddle Diddle." Mathers's expressive figures, in many moods, are effectively counter-pointed by touches of dramatic, or pensive, landscape. Pair this with the Opie/Sendak *I Saw Esau* for a feast of traditional rhymes. A delightfully idiosyncratic selection.

Nursery Rhymes; Mother Goose

E
P
Mavor, Salley. Pocketful of Posies: A Treasury of Nursery Rhymes. 64 pp. Houghton (Houghton Mifflin Trade and Reference Division) 2010. ISBN 978-0-618-73740-6.

Sixty-four nursery rhymes appear in an intricate tapestry of wool, felt, embroidery, beads, and every kind of needlework. With the constructions attentive to even the smallest details, the book is organized loosely from morning to night. The deftly pho-tographed needlework looks three-dimensional because the textures of the various media create shadows and encourage the eye to linger on every hand-sewn detail.

Nursery Rhymes

J
398.209
McDermott, Gerald. Monkey: A Trickster Tale from India. 32 pp. Harcourt (Harcourt Trade Publishers) 2011. ISBN 978-0-15-216596-3.

Crocodile informs Monkey that he plans to eat his heart. Quick-thinking Monkey replies, "What a pity. I left it up in the tree!" Despite his size, Crocodile is no match for ingenious Monkey. McDermott uses paint and paper collage, shredding the edg-es of the brown paper to create a furry look for Monkey. An opening note explains more about the story and the art.

Folktales/Myths/and Legends; Folklore—India; Tricksters; Animals—Monkeys; Animals—Crocodiles

J
398.2 Morpurgo, Michael. The Pied Piper of Hamelin. 64 pp. Candlewick 2011. ISBN 978-0-7636-4824-4. Illustrated by Emma Chichester Clark.

In Morpurgo's Hamelin Town, the children starve while the "rich and the greedy lived like kings and queens." Then comes a "plague of rats," who eat all the food and begin hunting in packs. Before its happy ending, the book is pretty grim; Clark's watercolors lighten the mood with lots of patterns and by depicting the rats as slightly comical.
Folktales/Myths/and Legends; Pied Piper of Hamelin (Legendary character); Folklore—Germany; Animals—Rats; Behavior—Greed; Musicians

E
P Pinkney, Jerry. Puss in Boots. 40 pp. Dial 2012. ISBN 978-0-8037-1642-1. series.

Pinkney provides sumptuous watercolor, gouache, and colored-pencil illustrations that place realistic natural elements side by side with ostentatious embellishments in the eighteenth-century clothing of the human characters. Aside from switching the story's usual ogre into a sorcerer, Pinkney sticks close to the source and uses his large pages, including a gatefold illustration, to great effect.
Folktales/Myths/and Legends; Animals—Cats; Folklore—France

E
P Pinkney, Jerry. The Tortoise & the Hare. 40 pp. Little 2013. ISBN 978-0-316-18356-7.

In Pinkney's brilliantly illustrated, nearly wordless Aesop fable, Tortoise's plodding journey across a desert landscape shows a host of critters native to the American Southwest cheering him on. The richly detailed pictures are lively and humorous, but what makes this retelling particularly ingenious is Pinkney's use of the "slow-and-steady" moral in a cumulative progression, both to recount the action and provide dramatic tension.
Folktales/Myths/and Legends; Folklore—Animals; Aesop; Animals—Tortoises; Animals—Rabbits; Fables; Southwest (U.S.); Deserts

O Stampler, Ann Redisch. The Rooster Prince of Breslov. 32 pp. Clarion 2010. ISBN 978-0-618-98974-4. Illustrated by Eugene Yelchin.

In this venerable Yiddish tale, a prince throws off his clothes and acts like a rooster. Cures fail, but an old man has a plan: by imitating the boy, he lures him into conversation. Stampler's witty storytelling nicely dramatizes such concepts as excess and compassion. Yelchin underlines the tale's subtlety and humor with apt caricatures rendered in minimal line and vivid gouache.
Folktales/Myths/and Legends; Folklore—Animals; Folklore—Jewish; Jews; Princes and princesses; Animals—Roosters

Stampler, Ann Redisch. The Wooden Sword: A Jewish Folktale from Afghanistan. 32 pp. Whitman 2012. ISBN 978-0-8075-9201-4. Illustrated by Carol Liddiment. The shah decides to test a poor Jewish shoemaker who is rich in faith. First he outlaws shoe repair, then prohibits water peddling (the resourceful man's second employ), and finally forces him to act as palace executioner. The shah gains wise council from the man, whose faith and ingenuity remain steadfast. Rich-hued paintings highlight the characters' goodheartedness while incorporating culture-specific details. Source note appended.

Folktales/Myths/and Legends; Kings, queens, and rulers; Folklore—Jewish; Afghanistan

* *

—FOCUS ON—

Folk and Fairy Tales Retold

Spin-offs

By Joy Fleishhacker

*A former SLJ staffer, Joy Fleishhacker is a freelance writer and youth
services librarian at Pikes Peak Library District in Colorado.*

* *

Fresh, funny, and boundary-breaking, these fractured fairy tales encourage children to revisit old friends, rethink familiar settings and scenarios, and let their imaginations soar. Splendidly illustrated and superbly told, they update, recast, and otherwise reinvent longtime favorites, providing clever and comical twists, reforging tried-and-true characterizations, and turning the traditional upside down.

Selected from an extensive and impressive body of work, the books featured here focus on well-known European folk and fairy tales and nursery rhymes. The titles have been chosen to represent an engaging array of storytelling styles and approaches, including poetry and epistle forms, first-person perspectives and omniscient narrations, as well as a magnificent variety of artistic mediums and methods. Not-to-be-forgotten classics have been mixed in with newer works, as the genre continues to evolve and expand. Appropriate for preschool and elementary-age youngsters, these offerings will enchant independent readers and bedazzle classroom and storytime audiences.

Firmly grounded in familiar fairy-tale territory, these spin-offs make great jump-off points for comparison and discussion. Children can explore variations in perspective and point of view, contemplate characterization and motivation, and identify similarities and differences from the original tales. Texts flavored with Spanish terms will delight bilingual readers and aid language instruction. These irresistible offerings might also motivate kids to write and/or illustrate their own versions of their favorite tales, spiced up, twisted, and reconfigured to suit their own sensibilities. And of course, the revved-up retellings incorporate the same universal themes and timeless wonder of the stories that inspired them, icing on an already-packed-with-child-appeal cake.

E
A

Ada, Alma Flor. Dear Peter Rabbit. 1994. RTE $18.99. ISBN 978-0-689-31850-4; ISBN 978-0-689-81289-7.

——. Yours Truly, Goldilocks. 1998. RTE $17.99. ISBN 978-0-689-81608-6; ISBN 978-0-689-84452-2.

——. With Love, Little Red Hen. 2001. RTE $17.99. ISBN 978-0-689-82581-1; ISBN 978-0-689-87061-3.

ea vol: illus. by Leslie Tryon. S & S/Atheneum. pap. $7.99.

K–Gr 4–The intertwining adventures of storybook characters are related through captivating communiqués penned by Baby Bear, Little Red Riding Hood, the Big Bad Wolf, and other residents of Hidden Forest. Tryon's watercolor illustrations depict this make-believe world with delectable detail and irresistible charm. Use in the classroom for letter-composition units, creative-writing projects, and character comparisons.

E
A

Ahlberg, Allan. Previously. illus. by Bruce Ingman. Candlewick. 2007. RTE $16.99. ISBN 978-0-7636-3542-8; pap. $6.99. ISBN 978-0-7636-5304-0.

PreS–Gr 3–Ahlberg retells seven well-known tales from end to beginning, smoothly interconnecting plot elements into a cohesive whole. The imagination-tickling adventure backtracks through the escapades of Goldilocks, who had earlier met a just-down-from-the-beanstalk boy named Jack, who had come from hill-tumbling with Jill, and so on. Fanciful sherbet-hued paintings depict the antics and keep the sequencing crystal clear.

Artell, Mike. Three Little Cajun Pigs. illus. by Jim Harris. Dial. 2006. RTE $16.99. ISBN 978-0-8037-2815-8.

K-Gr 4–Down in the "south Loo-siana" bayou, porcine siblings Trosclair, Thibodeaux, and Ulysses leave home to build their own abodes but soon find themselves stalked by a tail-thwacking gator with a taste for *couchon de lait* (roast pig). Sly humor, crackling Cajun-flavored couplets, and winning watercolor artwork make for laugh-out-loud fun.

Browne, Anthony. Me and You. illus. by author. Farrar. 2010. Tr $16.99. ISBN 978-0-374-34908-0.

PreS-Gr 3–Browne's discussion-provoking *Goldilocks* unfolds from parallel perspectives. A small bear narrates from bright-hued pages as he and his parents take a porridge-cooling stroll. Meanwhile, wordless sepia-toned illustrations show a fiery-haired girl getting separated from her mother, wandering their derelict neighborhood, and finding refuge at a cozy-looking house. Visual and thematic contrasts power the familiar plot with nuance and emotion.

Cole, Babette. Prince Cinders. illus. by author. Putnam. 1987. pap. $6.99. ISBN 978-0-6981-1554-5.

K-Gr 4–Left hearthside, a scrawny prince yearns to be more like his three big-and-hairy, slick-suit-wearing, palace-disco-going brothers. When a flaky fairy grants his wish, but mistakenly turns him into an outsize monkey sporting a red-and-white-striped swimsuit, he still manages to catch Princess Lovelypenny's eye and luck into a happy ending. An absolute hoot, with deadpan text and vivacious artwork.

Crews, Nina, retel. Jack and the Beanstalk. illus. by reteller. Holt/Christy Ottaviano Bks. 2011. RTE $16.99. ISBN 978-0-8050-8765-9.

PreS-Gr 3–Featuring a modern-day multicultural cast and city setting, Crews's colorful collage photos blend contemporary elements with once-upon-a-time wonder. In this updated, gently told version, Jack earns a jar of multicolored beans for doing chores, the not-too-scary giant and his wife set him to scrubbing spaghetti-crusted dishes, and the traditional ending is jazzed up with a surprise twist.

Duffy, Chris, ed. Nursery Rhyme Comics: 50 Timeless Rhymes from 50 Celebrated Cartoonists. First Second. 2011. Tr $18.99. ISBN 978-1-59643-600-8.

Gr 3 Up–An eye-dazzling anthology of chant-along classics, reinterpreted to suit contemporary sensibilities. Utilizing a variety of visual styles, mediums, and moods, children's book illustrators, comics creators, and other artists present exhilarating reimaginings that spin out inventive backstories, play fast and loose with the familiar, and celebrate the rhymes' glorious nonsensicality and time-tested appeal. A must-have volume.

Elya, Susan Middleton. Rubia and the Three Osos. illus. by Melissa Sweet. Hyperion/Disney. 2010. RTE $15.99. ISBN 978-1-4231-1252-5.

PreS-Gr 1–This jaunty *Goldilocks* retelling incorporates rhythmic rhymes, smoothly integrated Spanish terms, and a "fabuloso" ending in which Rubia makes amends to the family Oso and earns their friendship. Starring a golden-haired, cowgirl-boot-wearing darling and three packed-with-personality bears, Sweet's mixed-media paintings explode with action and humor. A tongue-pleasing read-aloud with bilingual zing.

Ernst, Lisa Campbell. The Gingerbread Girl Goes Animal Crackers. illus. by author. Dial. 2011. RTE $16.99. ISBN 978-0-525-42259-4.

Pres-Gr 2–Having outsmarted a greedy fox in *The Gingerbread Girl* (Dutton, 2006), the youngster returns for another madcap chase. This time she's the pursuer, dashing after a zoo full of cookie critters that have burst out of their box, through the door, and off to explore. Candy-coated artwork and boastful, buoyant rhymes add up to a sweet read-aloud treat.

Ernst, Lisa Campbell. Little Red Riding Hood: A Newfangled Prairie Tale. illus. by author. S & S. 1995. pap. $7.99. ISBN 978-0-689-82191-2.

K-Gr 3–Set in the contemporary Midwest, this tale introduces a red-hoodie-wearing, bicycle-riding protagonist who totes a basket of delicious-smelling muffins; a sneery-eyed wolf determined to steal Grandma's secret recipe for said treats; and a tough-as-nails, tractor-driving granny with no patience for lupine bullies. Humor and clever touches abound in the earth-toned artwork and bursting-with-action text.

Graves, Keith. Chicken Big. illus. by author. Chronicle. 2010. Tr $16.99. ISBN 978-0-8118-7237-9.

PreS-Gr 3–When a humongous yellow hatchling emerges from an egg, the bird-brained coop dwellers don't know what to make of him. However, after the feathered giant rescues the frantic flock from several comically exaggerated *Chicken-Little*-esque scenarios (and an egg-snatching fox), he earns true recognition and a place in their hearts. An eye-rolling yet heartwarming spoof, with appealingly over-the-top artwork.

Isadora, Rachel, retel. Rapunzel. illus. by reteller. Putnam. 2008. RTE $16.99. ISBN 978-0-399-24772-9.

K-Gr 4–Isadora adds a multicultural spin to this familiar tale by setting the action in a mythical African kingdom. In the dazzling verdant-hued spreads, Rapunzel's tower is woven from branches, she lets down beautiful flower-strewn dreadlocks, and the prince rides a gallant zebra. Other simply told, recast-in-Africa offerings by Isadora include *Hansel and Gretel* (2009) and *The Princess and the Pea* (2007, both Putnam).

Ketteman, Helen. Señorita Gordita. illus. by Will Terry. Albert Whitman. 2012. Tr $16.99. ISBN 978-0-8075-7302-0.

K-Gr 3–Hot out of the pan, a tasty-looking gordita (little fried tortilla) races "zip-zoom-zip" out the door and speeds past several hungry desert critters, bragging all the while, until she encounters cunning Búho (owl). A fast-paced, fun-filled read-aloud, spiced with Spanish terms, sizzling rhymes, and a sun-drenched Southwestern landscape. A glossary and recipe are appended.

Kimmel, Eric A. The Three Little Tamales. illus. by Valeria Docampo. Marshall Cavendish. 2009. RTE $17.99. ISBN 978-0-7614-5519-6.

K-Gr 3–Kimmel replaces the pigs with three just-steamed tamales who run away from a *taqueria* to save their cornhusk skins, cobble their *casitas* out of various materials (sagebrush, cornstalks, and cactus), and encounter a huffing and puffing Señor Lobo. Rhythmic bilingual refrains add zest, and lush-hued paintings portray the Southwestern setting and play up the humor.

Lowell, Susan. Cindy Ellen: A Wild Western Cinderella. illus. by Jane Manning. HarperCollins/Joanna Cotler Bks. 2000. Tr $17.99. ISBN 978-0-06-027446-7; pap. $6.99. ISBN 978-0-06-443864-3.

K-Gr 4–Lowell rustles up a sweet-natured bronco-busting cowgirl, a mean-as-a-rattlesnake stepmother, a gold-pistol-twirling fairy godmother, the handsome son of a cattle king, and the right-as-rain revelation that "Magic is plumb worthless without gumption." This rip-roaring retelling ropes in readers with old West lingo, colorful turns of phrase, and fun-and-fringe-spangled artwork.

E
M

Metzger, Steve. Detective Blue. illus. by Tedd Arnold. Scholastic/Orchard. 2011. RTE $16.99. ISBN 978-0-545-17286-8.

PreS-Gr 4–Little Boy Blue has a new gig as a gumshoe, and he's hot on the case when Miss Muffet mysteriously goes missing. Comic-book-style panels show the trench-coat-clad detective pounding the pavement, grilling nursery-rhyme denizens, and chasing clues. Readers will enjoy cracking the crime while hunting down numerous Mother Goose references presented in the color-drenched cartoons and in the noir-nuanced narrative.

O **Murray, Laura.** The Gingerbread Man Loose in the School. illus. by Mike Lowery. Putnam. 2011. RTE $16.99. ISBN 978-0-399-25052-1.

PreS-Gr 2–Freshly baked in a classroom oven, a charismatic cookie pops off the pan and chases after the students who whipped him up and left him behind, dashing through hallways and getting help from staff members along the way. Presenting effervescent rhymes and sprightly cartoons in large-size comic-book panels, this snicker-filled spin-off satisfies kids' appetite for the silly.

O **O'Malley, Kevin.** Animal Crackers Fly the Coop. illus. by author. Walker. 2010. Tr $16.99. ISBN 978-0-8027-9837-4; PLB $17.89. ISBN 978-0-8027-9838-1.

Gr 2-4–When a chicken who would rather tell jokes than make yolks sets out to follow her dream of becoming a "comedi-hen," she and three other quip-cracking animal runaways take on some robbers and find a way to put their talents to good use. O'Malley's slapstick send-up of *The Brementown Musicians* percolates with side-splitting puns and action-packed artwork.

O **Osborne, Mary Pope.** The Brave Little Seamstress. illus. by Giselle Potter. S & S/Anne Schwartz Bks. 2002. RTE $16.99. ISBN 978-0-6898-4486-7.

K-Gr 4–After dispatching seven flies with one fell swoop, a seamstress boldly embroiders "SEVEN WITH ONE BLOW!" on her coat. Misconstruing the phrase, a giant believes that she has slain seven giants, while a king assumes it was seven knights. Both present her with impossible challenges, but this plucky protagonist takes on each task with ingenuity and imagination. Wittily told and handsomely illustrated.

E
P

Palatini, Margie. The Three Silly Billies. illus. by Barry Moser. S & S. 2005. Tr $16.99. ISBN 978-0-6898-5862-8.

PreS-Gr 4–Confronted by a cantankerous toll-collecting troll, three fun-loving but flat-broke billy goats are prevented from driving their jalopy across a bridge—until they brainstorm a plan to pool their pennies with other traveling fairy-tale characters and give the grump his just deserts. Waggish wordplay, winsome watercolors, and droll contemporary details make for a riotous retelling.

E
P

Paul, Ann Whitford. Mañana, Iguana. illus. by Ethan Long. Holiday House. 2004. RTE $17.95. ISBN 978-0-8234-1808-4; pap. $6.99. ISBN 978-0-8234-1980-7.

K-Gr 3–Four amigos plan a welcome-spring fiesta, but when Iguana asks for help, Conejo (rabbit), Tortuga (turtle), and Culebra (snake) spout feeble excuses. On the big day, the hardworking lizard puts her foot down, and the lazy animals learn an upbeat lesson about friendship. A Southwest setting, sprinkled-with-Spanish-terms text, and desert-hued cartoon artwork give this lighthearted *Little Red Hen* takeoff plenty of punch. Audio version available from Live Oak Media.

J
S +
~~paper back~~

Scieszka, Jon. The Stinky Cheese Man and Other Fairly Stupid Tales. illus. by Lane Smith. Viking. 1992. Tr $17.99. ISBN 978-0-6708-4487-6.

Gr 2-6–Snidely narrated by Jack (of beanstalk fame), this spoof-filled send-up showcases such crackpot classics as "Chicken Licken," "Little Red Running Shorts," and "Cinderumpelstiltskin." Silly twists and comical comeuppances abound in the title's droll text and wry dark-toned collages as the characters and their antics spill out of their designated tales and create giggle-inducing mayhem. Audio version available from Audible.

E
paperback

Scieszka, Jon. The True Story of the 3 Little Pigs. illus. by Lane Smith. Viking. 1989. Tr $17.99. ISBN 978-0-6708-2759-6; pap $7.99. ISBN 978-0-1405-4451-0.

K-Gr 4 The much-maligned A. Wolf tells his side of the story, offering a deadpan account that chalks up the pig-felling tragedy to a quest for a cup of sugar and an ill-timed need to sneeze. This is the fractured fairy-tale gold standard, with tongue-in-cheek text and sophisticated artwork both darkly sinister and delightfully droll. DVD and audio versions available from Weston Woods.

O

Sierra, Judy. Tell the Truth, B. B. Wolf. illus. by J. Otto Seibold. Knopf. 2010. Tr $16.99. ISBN 978-0-375-85620-4; PLB $19.99. ISBN 978-0-375-95620-1.

PreS-Gr 3–Invited to the library to tell the story of how he met the three little pigs, the infamous wolf, now retired, spins a real whopper; however, his fairy-tale-folk audience remains unconvinced and the onetime villain ultimately admits his misdeeds and makes amends. The crackerjack text and stylishly exaggerated cartoons sparkle with humor and heart.

Singer, Marilyn. Mirror Mirror: A Book of Reversible Verse. illus. by Josée Masse. Dutton. 2010. RTE $16.99. ISBN 978-0-525-47901-7.
Gr 3-6–Juxtaposing Beauty with the Beast, Snow White with the wicked Queen, or Jack with the Giant, Singer uses "reverso" poems—selections that can be read forward or backward with the same wording but different meanings—to tell two sides of the same story. Inventive and enchanting, the poems are paired with mirror-image jewel-toned paintings that convey the dual perspectives. Audio version available from Live Oak Media.

Stanley, Diane. Goldie and the Three Bears. illus. by author. HarperCollins. 2003. pap. $7.99. ISBN 978-0-06-113611-5.
PreS-Gr 2–Goldie, a curly-haired modern girl who knows exactly what she likes, can't find a friend who's the perfect fit. However, when she gets off at the wrong school bus stop and wanders into a welcoming house, her ensuing adventure results in a companion who's "just right." Told with charming artwork, gentle humor, and true-to-the-audience insight.

Stimpson, Colin, retel. Jack and the Baked Beanstalk. illus. by reteller. Candlewick/Templar. 2012. Tr $15.99. ISBN 978-0-7636-5563-1.
K-Gr 4–Recast during the Depression with Jack and his mother running an almost-broke burger truck, this version features a magic vine that sprouts cans of tasty baked beans, a bored-with-counting-coins giant-size banker more lonesome than fearsome, and a satisfying money-doesn't-buy-happiness message. Sepia-toned artwork depicts the amiable characters and ebullient action with humor and cinematic flair.

Sturges, Philemon, retel. The Little Red Hen (Makes a Pizza). illus. by Amy Walrod. Dutton. 1999. Tr 16.99. ISBN 978-0-525-45953-8; pap. $6.99. ISBN 978-0-142-30189-0.
PreS-Gr 3–Colorful cut-paper collages introduce a chic-looking chick who wears platform shoes and lives in an apartment. When she asks her animal neighbors for help shopping and chopping, they're too busy playing to pitch in. However, the hen

never loses her cool, and her hot-out-of-the-oven pizza is served up along with a satisfying twist on the traditional ending.

E
W

Wiesner, David. The Three Pigs. illus. by author. Clarion. 2001. RTE $17.99. ISBN 978-0-618-00701-1. *Caldecott Display*
K-Gr 6–Blown "right out of the story" (and the picture panel) by the wolf's huffing and puffing, the first pig gathers his cohorts and embarks on a lively adventure that takes them off the beaten plot path, in and out of various tales (and styles of illustration), and beyond the boundaries of traditional storytelling conventions. Innovative, imagination-stirring, and thoroughly fun.

E
W

Wilcox, Leah. Waking Beauty. illus. by Lydia Monks. Putnam. 2008. RTE $16.99. ISBN 978-0-399-24615-9; pap. $6.99. ISBN 978-0142415382.
K-Gr 4–Prince Charming makes several harebrained attempts to awaken the snoring Beauty (hollering, water to face, shooting her from a cannon) before finally following the fairies' advice, though rather reluctantly—"One hundred years of morning breath./Wow! That could be the kiss of death!" Rollicking rhymes, frothy artwork, and kid-friendly humor make this parody a crowd-pleaser.

MEDIA PICKS
By Phyllis Levy Mandell

Chicken Little. DVD. 8 min. with tchr's. guide. Weston Woods. 2010. ISBN 978-0-545-29594-9: $59.95; CD, ISBN 978-0-545-29651-9: $12.95; CD with hardcover book, ISBN 978-0-545-29673-1: $29.95.
PreS-Gr 2–Ed Emberley and his daughter Rebecca collaborated on this delightful version (Roaring Brook, 2009) of the classic story. The google-eyed birdbrain hits the screen with a pop of bold colors and noisy onomatopoeia. Henny Penny, Lucky Ducky, Lucy Goosey, and Turkey Lurkey flit about worriedly as they follow Chicken Little in circles. Foxy Loxy invites the birds to stop and rest in a "warm, dark cave" situated just behind his sharp teeth—and the feather-brained fowls walk right in.

Goldilocks & Mother Goose and Friends. DVD. 30 min. with tchr's. guide. Nutmeg Media. 2010. ISBN 1-933938-67-6. $69.95.
PreS-Gr 2–Ruth Sanderson's retelling of *Goldilocks* (2009) begins as a more customary version with the golden-haired girl entering a bear family's cozy cottage and tasting porridge, sitting in chairs, and trying out the beds. She then takes the tale in a different direction by providing a lesson, a bit of tension, and the start of a friendship

between the bears and the girl. The realistic art brings this tale to life. In *Mother Goose and Friends* (2008, both Little, Brown), Sanderson's realistically rendered, gorgeous illustrations present a magical interpretation of both traditional and credited rhymes.

Lousy Rotten Stinkin' Grapes. by Margie Palatini. CD. 11:33 min. with hardcover book. Spoken Arts Media. 2010. ISBN 0-8045-4223-6. $29.95.
PreS-Gr 3–In this retelling of Aesop's fable *The Fox and the Grapes*, Fox unsuccessfully tries to reach a bunch of grapes hanging from a tree before deciding that they must be sour anyway. Barry Moser's watercolor illustrations are humorous and the perfect accompaniment to the text. Jim Brownold uses a variety of amusing voices to depict each of the woodland animals. Lively music and sound effects complement the text.

The Tortoise and the Hare. (Stories in Music Series). CD. approx. 54 min. with activity booklet. Maestro Classics. 2009. ISBN 978-1-932684-18-6. $16.98.
PreS-Gr 4–This entry in the series is presented by Stephen Simon and the London Philharmonic Orchestra. The simple Aesop fable, adapted by Bonnie Ward Simon and narrated by Yadu (Konrad Czynski), has been expanded to include press conferences, a pretzel vendor, and a French bistro. Simon's musical composition perfectly reflects the animals' movements and personalities.

ON THE WEB
For Students

Fractured Fairy Tales. www.readwritethink.org/files/resources/interactives/fairytales. ReadWriteThink/IRA/NCTE. (Accessed 6/21/14).
Gr 3 Up–Youngsters are invited to author their own re-imagined versions of three classic tales at this interactive site. Straightforward retellings of the stories are followed by guided templates highlighting characters, point of view, setting, and other elements that prompt users to envision their own changes. Related lesson plans are available at www.readwritethink.org/classroom-resources/student-interactives/fractured-fairy-tales-30062.html.

Story Magic. www.museumofplay.org/flash-games/story-magic. National Museum of Play/The Strong. Rochester, NY. (Accessed 6/21/14).
K-Gr 5–Children use a magic-wand icon to choose from five different story genres (including fairy tales); select and manipulate cartoon-style backgrounds, characters, animals, and objects to create a picture; write their own text; and then print out or save their masterpiece. A fun and user-friendly site based on a museum exhibit.

StoryPlace Elementary Library. www.storyplace.org/eel/eel.asp. Public Library of Charlotte & Mecklenburg County, NC. (Accessed 6/19/14).

K-Gr 4 This easy-to-use interactive site presents six "Topsy-Turvy" retellings of traditional tales, jazzed up with humor, eye-catching visuals, and updated scenarios. Children select characters and settings, name heroes and villains, and provide details for the stories, which then play out in a series of animated scenes (a combo of read-on-your-own text and character-narrated clips). A Spanish-language version is available at www.storyplace.org/sp/eel/other.asp.

For Educators

Fractured Fairy Tales & Fables with Jon Scieszka. teacher.scholastic.com/writewit/mff/fractured_fairy.htm. Scholastic. (Accessed 6/19/14).

Featuring the author's *The True Story of the 3 Little Pigs* (1989) and Aesop's-fables-inspired *Squids Will Be Squids* (1998, both Viking), this site offers book overviews, ideas for pre-reading discussion, and an enticing variety of creative classroom activities. Kids can also submit work to be published online, or browse other examples of student writing.

History

Ｏ Brown, Don. Gold! Gold from the American River! 64 pp. Roaring Brook/Flash Point 2011. ISBN 978-1-59643-223-9. Actual Times series.

Brown turns his earthy palette and voice to the California Gold Rush. His unique tone is both larger-than-life and precisely detailed, and the treatment suits his subject. Well-composed watercolors convey action and emotion, giving just enough detail and variety. Combining pathos and humor, the book communicates much with an engaging and brief text, making it a first-choice introduction to the subject. Websites. Bib. *North America; History, American—Gold rush; Gold; California*

Ｏ Brown, Don. Henry and the Cannons: An Extraordinary True Story of the American Revolution. 32 pp. Roaring Brook 2013. ISBN 978-1-59643-266-6. series.

In this follow-up to *Let It Begin Here!*, stylized watercolors heighten the drama and occasional humor of Henry Knox's mission to bring heavy cannon from Lake

Champlain forts to Washington's forces in 1776 Boston. The text hews closely to the record—except for one fact: Brown states, "Washington ached for cannon... But Washington had none," an unfortunate exaggeration of an otherwise "true story." Bib.

North America; Knox, Henry; History, American—Revolutionary War; Massachusetts; History, American—Colonial life; Soldiers

J 917.471

Brown, Marc. In New York. 40 pp. Knopf (Random House Children's Books) 2014. ISBN 978-0-375-86454-4. LE ISBN 978-0-375-96454-1.

Just about all of Manhattan's child-pleasing sites get a place in Brown's stupendously detailed gouache and watercolor pictures showing a little boy and his father touring NYC. The text is minimal but inviting ("wherever you walk in New York, you'll see a great parade of people passing by"); endpapers offer additional vignettes and facts. Appended information includes phone numbers and websites for the highlights.

Picture Books; New York (NY); Family—Father and son; Vacations; Voyages and travels

○ **Dowson, Nick.** North: The Amazing Story of Arctic Migration. 56 pp. Candlewick 2011. ISBN 978-0-7636-5271-5. Illustrated by Patrick Benson.

Dawson introduces readers to animals that migrate to the Arctic for the warmer summer months. Polar bears (year-round residents) are joined by whales from Mexico, herrings from Norway, and birds from as far away as Antarctica, among others. Luminous watercolor with pen and pencil illustrations capture the icy Arctic winters, the tundra's fleeting midsummer verdancy, and the migrating groups' gracefulness.

Polar Regions; Arctic regions; Migration; Animals—Arctic animals

○ **Evans, Shane W.** Underground. 32 pp. Roaring Brook/Porter 2011. ISBN 978-1-59643-538-4.

With dramatic images and minimal narrative, Evans projects a "we-are-there" experience of escaping slaves. White stars stand out against a richly textured midnight blue, as do the triangular whites of the fugitives' eyes and the bold white typeface itself; a golden sun rises on the final view of freedom. Adults discussing black history with five- and six-year-olds can use this visually intense evocation.

North America; Slavery; Fugitive slaves; African Americans; History, American—Underground Railroad

○ **Fern, Tracey.** Dare the Wind. 40 pp. Farrar/Ferguson 2014. ISBN 978-0-374-31699-
   0. Illustrated by Emily Arnold McCully.

Ellen Prentiss learned navigation on her father's trading schooner. When she and
her husband took command of a new clipper ship, heading from New York to the
California Gold Rush, Ellen smashed the record for shortest voyage around Cape
Horn. Fern's nautically infused text rolls with the waves, while McCully's ink and
watercolor illustrations reflect the resplendent blues and greens of vast oceans. Glos.
Individual Biographies; Sailors; Vehicles—Ships; Voyages and travels; History, American—
Gold rush; Oceans; Women—Sailors; Creesy, Eleanor

○ **Gandhi, Arun and Hegedus, Bethany.** Grandfather Gandhi. 48 pp. Atheneum (Simon
   & Schuster Children's Publishing) 2014. ISBN 9781-4424-2365-7. Illustrated
   by Evan Turk.

Mahatma Gandhi's grandson, Arun, who angers easily, feels he will never live up
to the Gandhi name. Gandhi explains that he, too, feels anger but has learned to
channel it for good. Unusual for its child-centered portrait of Gandhi, the graceful
narrative is matched by vivid mixed-media illustrations, rendered in watercolor, paper collage, cotton fabric, yarn, gouache, pencil, tea, and tinfoil.
Individual Biographies; Gandhi, Mahatma; Pacifists; Statesmen; India; Family—Grandfa-
thers; Emotions—Anger

J
940.1 **Macaulay, David.** Castle: How It Works. 32 pp. Square Fish/David Macaulay Studio
   2012. ISBN 978-1-59643-744-9. PE ISBN 978-1-59643-766-1. My Readers
   series. With Sheila Keenan.

Macaulay brings his signature brand of illustrated expository nonfiction to a younger audience. This book revisits a subject Macaulay has written about previously,
but the topics are here presented with the needs of developing readers in mind.
Abounding with Macaulay's sly, mischievous wit, the narrative invites readers to
envision themselves in the action; words and pictures work in tandem to effectively
weave information into this framework. Reading list, websites. Glos., ind.
Ancient and Medieval History; Castles; War

E
R **Rosenstock, Barb.** The Camping Trip That Changed America: Theodore Roosevelt, John
   Muir, and Our National Parks. 32 pp. Dial 2012. ISBN 978-0-8037-3710-5. Illus-
   trated by Mordicai Gerstein.

In 1903, Roosevelt asked Muir to take him camping in the Yosemite wilderness. By
the time the two reached Yosemite, Roosevelt had been persuaded to create "nation-

al parks, wildlife sanctuaries, and national forests." Rosenstock (as she explains in an author's note) has invented the dialogue here, but the ideas expressed are authentic. Gerstein brings his usual verve to the expedition. Bib.

North America; Yosemite National Park (CA); National parks and reserves; Muir, John; Presidents—United States; Roosevelt, Theodore; Camps and camping; Nature; Trees; Forests and forestry

○ **Rubbino, Salvatore.** A Walk in London. 40 pp. Candlewick 2011. ISBN 978-0-7636-5272-2.

A mother and daughter sightsee in London—watching the Changing of the Guard, touring St. Paul's Cathedral, riding a ferry down the Thames, etc. Playful yet realistic mixed-media illustrations, drawn from different perspectives, give readers a real sense of what it's like to visit the city. The pages are highly informative and jam-packed with things for young readers to view.

Europe; Toy and movable books; Family—Mother and daughter; London (England); Voyages and travels

○ **Van Rynbach, Iris and Shea, Pegi Deitz.** The Taxing Case of the Cows: A True Story About Suffrage. 32 pp. Clarion 2010. ISBN 978-0-547-23631-5. Illustrated by Emily Arnold McCully.

Faced with an unjust new tax, Julia and Abby Smith protested: since they couldn't vote, this was taxation without representation. After the sisters' cows are confiscated, the American Woman Suffrage Association, as well as newspapers nationwide, took up the story. Van Rynbach and Shea appealingly present the resourcefulness of two nineteenth-century women. McCully's illustrations show the aging sisters and their humorously vivacious cows.

North America; Connecticut; Voting; Women—Suffragists; Suffrage; Animals—Cows; Smith, Julia; Smith, Abby

○ **Winter, Jonah.** Born and Bred in the Great Depression. 40 pp. Random/Schwartz & Wade 2011. ISBN 978-0-375-86197-0. LE ISBN 978-0-375-96197-7. Illustrated by Kimberly Bulcken Root.

Winter retells his father's tales of growing up poor in East Texas. The family enjoyed good times "learning to love those things that didn't cost a single penny." This window into an era when people took scarcity for granted is effectively visualized in Root's pencil, ink, and watercolor art. Eight vintage snapshots of the family appear on the endpapers.

North America; Depression (Economic); Family—Father and son; Poverty; Family; Texas

–FOCUS ON–

American Indians

Getting It Right

By Debbie Reese

Debbie Reese is the editor of American Indians in Children's Literature.

At a conference held at the University of Wisconsin's Cooperative Children's Book Center in the early 1990s, James Ransome was asked why he had not illustrated any books with American Indian characters. His response, in short, was something to the effect of, "I haven't held their babies." He captured what it means to really engage with a people whose history and culture are not one's own. In this column, I've made an effort to include non-Native authors who have succeeded in forging the meaningful bonds to which Ransome alluded.

In writing about a culture that is not one's own, it is imperative to be able to make those connections. Good intentions are not enough to provide the history or perspective of Native peoples. Book research is not enough. Visits to reservations aren't enough, either. Real relationships with American Indians are vital in order to avoid romanticizing or denigrating various groups through stereotypical ideas and characters.

Teachers and librarians have been searching for multiple viewpoints for a long time. Some have been able to separate the good from the stereotypical, but growing a critical mass of individuals who will select books like the ones described here takes work. Order these titles. Read them. Study them. We can all be better informed and assist readers as they make truly meaningful connections.

○ **Edwardson, Debby Dahl.** Whale Snow. illus. by Annie Patterson. Charlesbridge. 2003. RTE $15.95. ISBN 978-1-57091-393-8; pap. $7.95. ISBN 978-1-57091-394-5. K-Gr 2–Through the teachings of his grandma, family, and community, a young Inupiaq boy develops his understanding of traditional ways of life and how deeply the culture is shaped by his community's coexistence with whaling and the environment. The watercolor palette effectively captures the cold of the northern landscape and the warmth of the people. An Inupiaq edition is available on the author's website, www.debbydahledwardson.com.

Erdrich, Louise. Chickadee. illus. by author. HarperCollins/ Harper. 2012. Tr $16.99. ISBN 978-0-06-057790-2; lib. ed. $17.89. ISBN 978-0-06-057791-9; ebk. $6.99. ISBN 978-0-06-219007-9.

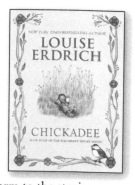

Gr 3-8–In this, the fourth book in the "Birchbark House" series, Omakayas is now grown and the mother of eight-year-old twin boys, one of whom is kidnapped. As Chickadee and his family try to find one another, Erdrich eloquently imparts Ojibwe stories, history, and knowledge, and, as in the previous books, her own illustrations add charm to the stories.

Francis, Lee DeCora. Kunu's Basket: A Story from Indian Island. illus. by Susan Drucker. Tilbury. 2012. Tr $16.95. ISBN 978-0-88448-330-4.

K-Gr 2–With the help of his caring and patient grandfather, Kunu, a contemporary Penobscot boy, overcomes his struggles to learn how to make the baskets Penobscot men have crafted for generations. In the process, he learns a bit about Penobscot history, too. Illustrations are gentle in tone, reflecting the relationship between Kunu and his grandfather.

Galvan, Glenda. Chikasha Stories, Volume One: Shared Spirit. illus. by Jeannie Barbour. Chickasaw Press. 2011. Tr $36. ISBN 978-1-935684-04-6.

Gr 2-4–Why do skunks smell bad? The answer, from the Chickasaw perspective, is conveyed in one of five traditional stories presented with text in English and Chickasaw. Whimsical illustrations rendered in vivid colors invite a chuckle as the stories unfold. Notes from the author, illustrator, and people who provided the Chickasaw text provide insights into the publication of the series, which includes *Chikasha Stories, Volume Two: Shared Voices* (Chickasaw, 2012). A third volume was published in October 2013.

Nelson, S. D. Greet the Dawn: The Lakota Way. illus. by author. South Dakota State Historical Society. 2012. Tr $18.95. ISBN 978-0-9845041-6-9.

K-Gr 5–Nelson takes readers through a day in the life of Lakota children. Like any kids, they wear jeans and sneakers as they ride a yellow bus to school, but their traditional Lakota ways are part of that day, too. Nelson's distinctive style of illustration blends the realistic here-and-now with representations of the spiritual dimensions of Lakota life.

Nelson, S. D., retel. Buffalo Bird Girl: A Hidatsa Story. illus. by reteller. Abrams. 2012.

RTE $19.95. ISBN 978-1-4197-0355-3.
Gr 3-6–With a mix of photographs and interpretive artwork, Nelson's biography of Buffalo Bird Woman (1839-1932) is a comprehensive and unflinching look at how the Hidatsa people and their nation were impacted by Native and non-Native nations, while still being mindful of the book's audience. Notes provide teachers with information to supplement the content.

Sneve, Virginia Driving Hawk. The Christmas Coat: Memories of My Sioux Childhood. illus. by Ellen Beier. Holiday House. 2011. RTE 16.95. ISBN 978-0-8234-2134-3.
Gr 1-4–Sneve offers a look into how her childhood was infused with traditional Lakota ways, but enriched, too, by the Episcopal church on her reservation. From the toys in Santa's bag to the setting for the autobiographical story, Beier's research is evident in the detail of her outstanding illustrations.

Tingle, Tim. Saltypie: A Choctaw Journey from Darkness into Light. illus. by Karen Clarkson. Cinco Puntos. 2010. Tr $17.95. ISBN 978-1-933693-67-5.

K-Gr 5–Tingle shares his family history and their experience with racism. Clarkson's illustrations quietly capture the sadness and joy of Tingle's words as he recounts how his grandmother lost and eventually regained her sight. The story and the author's intimate and heartfelt notes provide multiple opportunities for readers to move from darkness into light.

Uluadluak, Donald. Kamik: An Inuit Puppy Story. illus. Qin Leng. Inhabit Media. 2013. pap. $10.95. ISBN 978-1-9270-9511-9.
Gr 1-4–How to train a puppy, or what not to do when training a puppy, is the theme of this delightful picture book. From his grandfather's stories, Jake learns what his pup must be taught as it takes its place as a sled dog in an Inuit community. Leng's exquisite and lively illustrations capture the exuberance of puppyhood.

DIGITAL PICKS

Apps

Anompa: Chickasaw Language Basic. Chickasaw Nation. Thornton Media. 2011. Version: 1.1. iOS, requires 3.2 or later. Free.
Gr 3 Up–Common words (snow) and Chickasaw-specific words and phrases ("The Chickasaw people will dance, until the world ends.") are shown in English, with the Chickasaw word or phrase presented in print and audio. Content is arranged in more than 20 different categories, two of which are hymns and videos.

Bramble Berry Tales-The Story of Kalkalilh: Book One. Rival Schools Media Design. Loud Crow Interactive. 2013. Version: 1.2. iOS, requires 5.0 or later. $2.99. Android, requires 2.3.3 and up. Version 1.0. $2.99.
PreS Up–Lily and Thomas visit their grandparents in this captivating storybook. While there, their grandfather tells them a traditional Coast Salish story about Kalkalilh. The text and audio can be read and played in English, French, Spanish, or Squamish, and interactive features provide background for the Squamish information in the story.

Ojibway. Ogoki Learning Systems. Darrick Glen Baxter and Arlene Mousseau. 2012. Version 1.4. iOS, requires 5.0 or later. Free. Android, requires 2.0.1 and up. Version 1.0. Free.
Gr 3 Up–Provides information about Ojibway people in four categories: Language, Syllabics, People, and Maps. The Language category has 13 sections that show buttons with English words or phrases. The Ojibway translation is provided in audio. In the Maps category, users can view a map of North America, changing it to view International Borders, Ojibway Territory, and Ojibway Indian Bands/Nations.

Websites

Chickasaw Kids. www.chickasawkids.com. Chickasaw Nation. (Accessed 6/19/14).
K Up–An interactive tour of the Chickasaw White House, listed on the National Register of Historic Sites, provides information about Chickasaw history, culture, and language through games, activities, and videos. Some (coloring sheets) are geared for young children while others (biographies) are better suited for older children.

Eds. Note: The full version of "Getting It Right" is available online at http://ow.ly/yevKg

—FOCUS ON—

The Titanic

Unsinkable

By Barbara Wysocki

Barbara Wysocki is the retired codirector
of Children's Services at the Cora J. Belden Library in Rocky Hill, CT.

April 2012 marked the centennial of the sinking of the *Titanic* off the coast of Newfoundland. Even after 100 years, the disastrous loss of the White Star Line's premier ship continues to fascinate. Over the course of 10-plus decades, the calamity has inspired a Broadway show, multiple books, and several movies. But why do students remain interested?

Dr. Robert D. Ballard, the president of the Sea Research Foundation's Institute for Exploration in Mystic, CT, found the *Titanic* on the seafloor in 1985. In an interview on immersionlearning.org, a website devoted to ocean-science education, Ballard says, "To children, it's the stuff of legend—heroes, villains and above all adventure." Commenting on the vessel's enduring appeal when he returned to it in 2004, Ballard adds, "Everyone can relate to someone's story from the ship," and he mentions plucky survivor Molly Brown and brave Ida Straus, who left her lifeboat to join her husband as the ship sank.

FICTION

Crisp, Marty. Titanicat. illus. by Robert Papp. Sleeping Bear. 2008. Tr $17.95. ISBN 978-1-58536-355-1.

K-Gr 4–A Belfast boy signs on to care for the ship's cat as the *Titanic* sails to America. During the preparatory trials, he diligently looks after the feline mother and her kittens, but when the cat abandons ship with her young in Southampton, he follows. Large single- and two-page paintings portray the boy's lucky choice with hushed beauty.

Gunderson, Jessica. Your Life as a Cabin Attendant on the Titanic. (The Way It Was Series.) illus. by Rachel Dougherty. Picture Window. 2012. PLB $25.99. ISBN

978-1-4048-7158-8; pap. $7.95. ISBN 978-1-4048-7248-6.

Gr 3-5–This Upstairs Downstairs approach follows an imagined female cabin attendant while revealing that most of the crew never got their final wages and that few were women because they were considered bad luck. Occasionally exaggerated cartoon images are interspersed with facts and humorous observations.

Lassieur, Allison. Can You Survive the Titanic?: An Interactive Survival Adventure. (You Choose: Survival Series). Capstone. 2011. PLB $30.65. ISBN 978-1-4296-6586-5; pap. $6.95. ISBN 978-1-4296-7351-8.

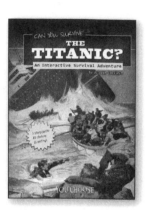

Gr 3-5–Through the eyes of the ship's assistant surgeon, a governess from the upper crust, and a 12-year-old boy from third class, readers follow multiple post-collision actions that save or cost lives. Short, specific sections move to final, sometimes sad, resolutions. A chapter relating the book's true-life basis and a few photos widen the appeal.

NONFICTION

Adams, Simon. Titanic. (Eyewitness Books Series). DK. 2009. Tr $16.99. ISBN 978-0-756-65036-0.

Gr 3-8–Complemented by a bonus clip art CD and a poster with views of the ship, the information- and illustration-intensive two-page entries touch on the "Captain and crew," "A deadly collision," "End of an era," and other related subjects. Perfect for an overview or for report topics.

Benoit, Peter. The Titanic Disaster. (A True Book: Disasters Series). Children's Press. 2011. PLB $28. ISBN 978-0-531-20627-0; pap. $6.95. ISBN 978-0-531-28996-9.

Gr 3-5–Intriguing text and excellent photos and illustrations chronicle the historic tragedy, from the ship's launch to post-disaster reports. The book includes a brief discussion of the shipwreck's discovery by Dr. Ballard as well as concerns about recent negative effects of tourism at the site.

Brewster, Hugh. Inside the Titanic. illus. by Ken Marschall. Little, Brown. 1997. Tr $19.99. ISBN 978-1-864-48382-6.

Gr 1-5–Like the ship they represent, giant color spreads, many with detailed cutaway views, showcase the basics of the voyage and the rescue, as experienced by two real-life families, one in first class and another in third. Small black-and-white photos of travelers, workers, and artifacts are interspersed. Visually valuable for older students as well.

J
3 87, 2 **Brown, Don.** All Stations! Distress! April 15, 1912: The Day the Titanic Sank. illus. by author. Roaring Brook. 2008. Tr $17.99. ISBN 978-1-59643-222-2; pap. $7.99. ISBN 978-1-596-43222-2

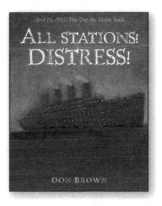

Gr 3 5 Brown opens his riveting narrative with information about the Belfast shipyard where the *Titanic* was built and the Southampton harbor from which it launched. Carefully selected quotes, soft-edged watercolor illustrations, and captivating descriptions detail the ship's dramatic final hours.

O **Denenberg, Barry.** Titanic Sinks!: Experience the Titanic's Doomed Voyage in This Unique Presentation of Fact and Fiction. Viking. 2011. Tr $19.99. ISBN 978-0-670-01243-5.

Gr 3 Up–Primary-source articles from the cleverly constructed but fictional magazine *Modern Times* delve into the *Titanic's* construction, Captain Smith, and the voyage through an imagined correspondent's journal and the real tales of survivors. Staff statistics, a dining menu, and the gymnasium schedule add valuable detail. Oversize, and with captivating photos, this title is ideal for reports and pleasure reading. Younger students will find the text challenging, but delight in the abundant images.

J
387. 2
+ E
Paperback
Donnelly, Judy. Titanic: Lost...and Found. illus. by Keith Kohler. Random. 1987. pap. $3.99. ISBN 978-0-394-88669-5; ebook $3.99. ISBN 978-0-307-56067-4.

Gr 2-4–Incorporating a mix of drama and information well suited for reading aloud, Donnelly relates the facts with a storyteller's flair as her easy-reader text begins at the launch, moves to the collision, and concludes with the modern exploration of the ship's wreckage. Softly toned illustrations complement the account.

J
3 87, 2 **Dubowski, Mark.** Titanic: The Disaster That Shocked the World. DK. 1998. Reprinted 2012. Tr $14.99. ISBN 978-0-7566-9083-0; pap. $3.99. ISBN 978-0-7566-9082-3.

Gr 1-3–Ticking off important events by day and time from launch to rescue, this easy reader reveals a kidnapping, explains how the ship sank, and generally keeps up the disaster intensity. Authentic black-and-white photos and labeled color illustrations, several with cutaway views, add valuable details in this well-designed book.

Dunn, Joe. The Titanic. illus. by Ben Dunn. ABDO/Magic Wagon. 2007. PLB $28.50. ISBN 978-1-602-70079-6.
Gr 3–5–Organized in short chapters, the book describes the ship's voyage in easy-to-follow fact boxes and related dialogue, both factual and imagined. Clean, uncomplicated color artwork matches the graphic-novel presentation. Likely to encourage reluctant readers.

Lorbiecki, Marybeth. Escaping Titanic: A Young Girl's True Story of Survival. illus. by Korey S. Heinzen. Picture Window. 2012. PLB $26.65. ISBN 978-1-4048-7143-4; pap. $8.95. ISBN 978-1-4048-7235-6.
Gr 3–5–On her way home from India with her mother and two younger siblings, preteen Ruth Becker boarded the *Titanic*. Separated from her family, she was the last one on lifeboat 13. Ominous, dark paintings add to the drama of this short, fact-based story that conveys the fear and confusion that one family experienced.

Shoulders, Debbie & Michael. T Is for Titanic: A Titanic Alphabet. illus. by Gijsbert van Frankenhuyzen. Sleeping Bear. 2011. Tr $17.95. ISBN 978-1-58536-176-2.
Gr 1–5–From "A" for the anatomy of the ship to third-class passenger Zimmerman, these oversize, appealingly detailed single pages and spreads use short rhymes and brief but sophisticated explanations to depict aspects of the *Titanic*. An online teacher's guide with downloadable activity sheets adds across-the-curriculum options.

Spedden, Daisy Corning Stone. Polar, the Titanic Bear. Little, Brown. 2001. pap. $10.99. ISBN 978-0-316-80909-2.
Gr 2 Up–In 1913, an American heiress wrote this travel memoir told through the eyes of a toy bear. Sharing first-person details about her family, including her young son, she recounts their experiences. Family photos and painted illustrations add to the representation of a wealthy Edwardian lifestyle. A valuable background resource for older students.

Stewart, Melissa. Titanic. National Geographic. 2012. PLB $17.99. ISBN 978-1-426-31060-7; pap. $3.99. ISBN 978-1-426-31059-1.
Gr 2–4–A good introduction for younger readers, this overview opens with the discovery of the ship's wreckage, then briefly delineates ship and voyage facts, history,

personalities, tragic events, and first-person quotes with photos, drawings, and text balloons. Stewart also addresses concerns about the ship's current status.

Eds. Note: The full version of "Unsinkable" is available online at http://ow.ly/yezb4.

Literature & Poetry

Ahlberg, Allan. Everybody Was a Baby Once: And Other Poems. 64 pp. Candlewick 2010. ISBN 978-0-7636-4682-0. Illustrated by Bruce Ingman.

This collection of short poems, some new, some recycled, is unified by Ingman's creation of a friendly little town of row-houses where children and witches, and dancing sausages and animated bathtubs live in (mostly) genial coexistence. Ahlberg's naughtiness and pinches of melancholy pair with Ingman's homely line drawings to keep the whole thing safely on the wry side of cute.

Poetry; Humorous poetry

Christelow, Eileen. What Do Authors and Illustrators Do?: Two Books in One. 78 pp. Houghton 2013. ISBN 978-0-547-97260-2.

Christelow's jaunty, informative books *What Do Authors Do?* (1995) and *What Do Illustrators Do?* (1999) are bound together in one useful volume. Clear cartoon panel dialogues between two author and illustrator characters—and each one's dog or cat—elucidate bookmaking's creative process from kernel-of-an-idea to bound book. A new "P.S.—From the (Real) Author-Illustrator" touches on digital art; activities encouraging creativity are appended.

Authors; Books and reading; Illustrators; Publishers and publishing

Coombs, Kate. Water Sings Blue: Ocean Poems. 32 pp. Chronicle 2012. ISBN 978-0-8118-7284-3. Illustrated by Meilo So.

The creatures and allure of the sea are captured in twenty-three poems with as many moods as the sea itself. Shark, sea turtle, coral, or whale, So's sea creatures

are all engaging, but it's the ocean itself that stars in her beautiful art, whether in translucent underwater greens, intense blue against a dazzling white horizon, or simply as splashes of color and light.
Poetry; Oceans; Animals—Marine animals

Florian, Douglas. Poetrees. 48 pp. Simon/Beach Lane 2010. ISBN 978-1-4169-8672-0. Swiveling his pages ninety degrees for tree-tall vertical spreads, the popular poet-illustrator celebrates the utility and diversity of trees in thirteen poems on a variety of species, plus five on such features as seeds, roots, and bark. Handsome, freely rendered multimedia art, more evocative than representational, illustrates the quirky poems.
Poetry; Trees; Humorous poetry

Florian, Douglas. Shiver Me Timbers!: Pirate Poems & Paintings. 32 pp. Simon/Beach Lane 2012. ISBN 978-1-4424-1321-4. Illustrated by Robert Neubecker. series.
Using stereotypical pirate-speak, each poem explores a familiar aspect of pirate lore and takes it to a new level of rhythm and rhyme. Final lines are calculated to evoke a chuckle, sometimes veering into the deliciously disgusting. Neubecker's digitally colored India-ink illustrations play well with Florian's verse, which is balanced between light gore and outright silliness.
Poetry; Humorous poetry; Pirates

Florian, Douglas. UnBEElievables: Honeybee Poems and Paintings. 32 pp. Simon/Beach Lane 2012. ISBN 978-1-4424-2652-8.
Working in gouache, colored pencils, and collage on paper bags, Florian evokes the world of bees with repetitive patterning that cleverly references their honeycombs and the fields of flowers they frequent as well as the bees themselves. His humorous rhythmic verse, too, echoes bee behavior, as much with sound as with sense. A paragraph of more straightforward facts elucidates each spread. Bib.
Poetry; Environment—Ecology; Animals—Bees; Humorous poetry

Franco, Betsy. A Dazzling Display of Dogs. 40 pp. Tricycle (Ten Speed Press) 2011. ISBN 978-1-58246-343-8. LE ISBN 978-1-58246-387-2. Illustrated by Michael Wertz.
As in *A Curious Collection of Cats*, Franco's concrete poems celebrate animals complete with lovable quirks and downright silliness. Wertz's stylish digital illustra-

tions pop with color and capture the personality of each dog variety, from pug to maltipoo. The combination of funny poems and goofy dogs makes for a great gift book—and a sneaky way to inject poetry into someone's life.

Poetry; Poetry—Concrete poems; Humorous poetry; Animals—Dogs; Pets

J 590

Gibson, Amy. Around the World on Eighty Legs. 56 pp. Scholastic 2011. ISBN 978-0-439-58755-6. Illustrated by Daniel Salmieri.

This collection of animal poems opens with a map of the world; the fifty-plus poems, in a variety of forms, are arranged geographically by region. Funny wordplay matches up with amusing illustrations in watercolor, gouache, and colored pencil that depict each animal accurately but with a twinkle of personality. A selection of further interesting animal facts is appended.

Poetry; Animals; Humorous poetry

Gray, Rita. One Big Rain: Poems for Rainy Days. 32 pp. Charlesbridge 2010. ISBN 978-1-57091-716-5. Illustrated by Ryan O'Rourke.

Illustrated with an appropriate palette of grays, blues, and olive greens, this anthology of twenty poems quietly celebrates rain. On the whole, the poems favor imagery over bouncy rhyme, with the pictures adding just enough snap to keep things from becoming too sleepy. The book design is invitingly small, and the poems' placement on the pages is clean and eye-pleasing.

Poetry Collections; Weather—Rain; Seasons

Greenfield, Eloise. The Great Migration: Journey to the North. 32 pp. HarperCollins/Amistad 2011. ISBN 978-0-06-125921-0. Illustrated by Jan Spivey Gilchrist.

Following an informative introduction, poignant poems tell the story of the Great Migration of African Americans from the South to the cities of the North. Many of the pieces give voice to unnamed travelers' thoughts; Greenfield explores the heart of each person. Gilchrist's cut paper, ephemera, paint, and processed photographs create collages, adding the right air of seriousness and history to the poetry.

Poetry; African Americans; Southern States; History, American

J 811.008

Hoberman, Mary Ann. Forget-Me-Nots: Poems to Learn by Heart. 144 pp. Little/Tingley 2012. ISBN 978-0-316-12947-3. Illustrated by Michael Emberley.

Hoberman has selected more than 120 poems that are good choices for memorization. Divided into eleven sections, the collection is a treasure trove of the familiar and the fresh. Emberley's watercolor, pastel, and pencil pictures both embellish and

illustrate the poems. A wonderful gift book for poetry lovers, but even children who have never considered memorizing a poem will find much to love here. Ind.
Poetry Collections; Memory

E
H
Hoberman, Mary Ann. You Read to Me, I'll Read to You: Very Short Fables to Read To-gether. 32 pp. Little/Tingley 2010. ISBN 978-0-316-04117-1. Illustrated by Michael Emberley.
This reliable series gets a refreshing variation, with its signature phrase ("You read to me! / I'll read to you!") replaced by pithy rhyming morals. The thirteen fables are mostly familiar; their traditional structure makes them a canny choice for the col-or-coded poems for two voices. Hoberman is really the master of unforced rhyme, and Emberley's pencil-and-watercolor illustrations are consistently spry.
Poetry

Hopkins, Lee Bennett. Dizzy Dinosaurs: Silly Dino Poems. 48 pp. HarperCollins/ Harper 2011. ISBN 978-0-06-135839-5. PE ISBN 978-0-06-135841-8. Il-lustrated by Barry Gott.
Nineteen dinosaur poems plus a pronunciation guide to dinosaur names make up this easy reader collection; as promised in the subtitle, the pieces poke a little dino-fun. Gott's paintings exaggerate the animals comically, giving the prehistoric critters a vari-ety of bright colors and showing their disparate sizes. Youngsters will enjoy the humor of these creatures set amidst ordinary modern life.
Poetry Collections; Prehistoric life—Dinosaurs; Humorous poetry

Hopkins, Lee Bennett. Nasty Bugs. 32 pp. Dial 2012. ISBN 978-0-8037-3716-7. Il-lustrated by Will Terry.
Children's poets such as Alice Schertle, J. Patrick Lewis, and Douglas Florian write about the yuckiest of insects, including lice, ticks, bedbugs, stink bugs, and, of course, the venerable cockroach. The poets use a variety of styles while maintaining a consistently humorous tone. If the words don't get your skin crawling, the vividly colored illustrations will. Three pages of facts are appended.
Poetry Collections; Animals—Insects; Humorous poetry

Janeczko, Paul B. Firefly July: A Year of Very Short Poems. 48 pp. Candlewick 2014. ISBN 978-0-7636-4842-8. Illustrated by Melissa Sweet.
Sweet's child-friendly mixed-media illustrations—loosely rendered, collage-like assemblages in seasonal palettes—enhance the thirty-six excellent poems show-

cased on the book's ample spreads. As brief as three lines or a dozen words, most of the verses are by familiar poets (Carl Sandburg, Langston Hughes), including those known for their children's verse (Alice Schertle, Charlotte Zolotow). A fine addition to the seasonal poetry shelf.

Poetry Collections; Seasons

Katz, Susan. The President's Stuck in the Bathtub: Poems About the Presidents. 64 pp. Clarion 2012. ISBN 978-0-547-18221-6. Illustrated by Robert Neubecker.

In forty-three poems, Katz gives each of our U.S. presidents their due, with footnotes providing a more complete discussion of the highlighted event or character trait. Neubecker's illustrations emphasize the playful tone without deconstructing the verse. Appended is a list of presidents with their dates in office; birth and death dates; nicknames; a "first" accomplishment of the man or office; and a famous quote.

Poetry; Presidents—United States; Humorous poetry

Kinerk, Robert. Oh, How Sylvester Can Pester!: And Other Poems More or Less About Manners. 32 pp. Simon/Wiseman 2011. ISBN 978-1-4169-3362-5. Illustrated by Drazen Kozjan.

Kinerk covers all sorts of etiquette-related behavior (including adults forgetting to use the manners they demand of children) in poems that are varied and funny; along the way readers should also find themselves picking up a tip or two. Kozjan's digital illustrations look slightly retro and feature a multicultural cast of characters, each with spindly limbs and a highly expressive face.

Poetry; Manners; Humorous poetry

Levine, Gail Carson. Forgive Me, I Meant to Do It: False Apology Poems. 80 pp. Harper-Collins/Harper 2012. ISBN 978-0-06-178725-6. LE ISBN 978-0-06-178726-3. Illustrated by Matthew Cordell.

Levine unapologetically riffs on William Carlos Williams's poem "This Is Just to Say" in this collection of light verse that shows readers there's a lot more to be un-sorry about besides purloined chilled plums. Accompanied by an appropriately scruffy, subversive cartoon, each poem mimics Williams's structure. Levine's spirited encouragement of readers to write their own false apology poems will likely be heeded.

Poetry; Humorous poetry; Williams, William Carlos

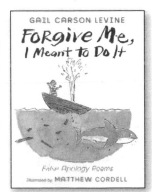

Lewis, J. Patrick. World Rat Day: Poems About Real Holidays You've Never Heard Of. 40 pp. Candlewick 2013. ISBN 978-0-7636-5402-3. Illustrated by Anna Raff.

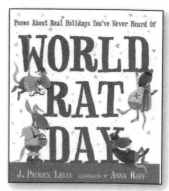

Twenty-two obscure but entertaining holidays get their own poems, each one funny, playful, and even instructive. The poems vary in length and style, with a concrete poem in the shape of a flamingo for Pink Flamingo Day and five limericks in honor of May 12, Limerick Day. Raff's ink washes and drawings feature animals with lots of personality.
Poetry; Holidays; Humorous poetry

Lyon, George Ella. All the Water in the World. 40 pp. Atheneum/Jackson (Simon & Schuster Children's Publishing) 2011. ISBN 978-1-4169-7130-6. Illustrated by Katherine Tillotson.

Lyon celebrates the essence of life itself in a lyrical poem about the water cycle. In sweeping, digitally rendered art resembling watercolor and collage, Tillotson creates luxuriant ocean swirls and pelting streaks of rain. It's a familiar subject but a vital one, to which author and illustrator bring a passion and artistry that give it the power of story.
Poetry; Water; Environment—Conservation—Natural resources; Water cycle

Prelutsky, Jack. Stardines Swim High Across the Sky and Other Poems. 40 pp. Greenwillow (HarperCollins Children's Books Group) 2013. ISBN 978-0-06-201464-1. LE ISBN 978-0-06-201465-8. Illustrated by Carin Berger. series.

Ingenious book design pairs with inventive poetry to feature unusual critters such as Fountain Lions, Braindeer, and Slobsters. The fun comes in the perfect but unexpected matches Prelutsky makes, such as the Jollyfish, "radiant, / Ebullient blobs of mirth." Berger incorporates found objects, aged paper, and other miscellanea to tag and label the various beasts. The total effect is both whimsical and fascinating.
Poetry; Imagination

Raczka, Bob. Guyku: A Year of Haiku for Boys. 48 pp. Houghton (Houghton Mifflin Trade and Reference Division) 2010. ISBN 978-0-547-24003-9. Illustrated by Peter H. Reynolds.

Focusing on nature and seasons, each of Raczka's twenty-four haiku captures with

amazing economy specific moments of a boy's life. Reynolds depicts the characters' glee and energy as well as natural elements in just a few deft lines. The pages are clean white, the book's shape is small and square, and each poem is accompanied by a delicate and funny two-color illustration.
Poetry; Poetry—Haiku; Seasons; Nature

Rosen, Michael J. The Hound Dog's Haiku and Other Poems for Dog Lovers. 56 pp. Candlewick 2011. ISBN 978-0-7636-4499-4. Illustrated by Mary Azarian.
Twenty haiku portray a range of dog breeds, from Pembroke Welsh Corgi to Samoyed to Border Collie. Accompanying the poems are Azarian's woodcut illustrations, printed in black and hand-colored with acrylics. The meticulously detailed woodcuts sturdily capture every dog and its setting, whether indoors or out, and echo the essential image expressed in each of the poems.
Poetry; Animals—Dogs; Pets; Poetry—Haiku

Sidman, Joyce. Dark Emperor & Other Poems of the Night. 32 pp. Houghton (Houghton Mifflin Trade and Reference Division) 2010. ISBN 978-0-547-15228-8. Illustrated by Rick Allen.
Sidman celebrates the world that comes alive after dark; each poem is accompanied by an informative paragraph that also exhibits her flair for language. The dark lines of Allen's skillful lino cut prints make the perfect accompaniment to a book of night poems, their subtle colors encouraging readers to seek out the creatures slowly, just as eyes become accustomed to the dark. Glos.
Poetry; Animals—Nocturnal animals; Night

Sidman, Joyce. Ubiquitous: Celebrating Nature's Survivors. 40 pp. Houghton (Houghton Mifflin Trade and Reference Division) 2010. ISBN 978-0-618-71719-4. Illustrated by Beckie Prange.
As Sidman points out, "99 percent of all species that have ever existed are now extinct." In her fourteen poems, the survivors range from bacteria to us, from ancient (mollusks) to newcomers (crows). The pieces vary in tone and form; facts are supplemented in prose. In the entrancing illustrations, Prange's bold linocuts are drenched in vivid watercolor. Timeline, websites. Glos.
Poetry; Nature; Animals; Biology

J
811

Silverstein, Shel. Every Thing On It. 202 pp. HarperCollins/Harper 2011. ISBN 978-0-06-199816-4. LE ISBN 978-0-06-199817-1.
This posthumously published volume of 140-plus poems is every bit as good as Silverstein's earlier collections. The book is not just laugh-out-loud funny but demands to be read aloud. Drawings add immeasurably to the entertainment, often providing the punch line. With its share of the slightly creepy, the slightly naughty, and the slightly gross—and also some poignant pieces—the volume has depth and humor.
Poetry; Humorous poetry

○ **Singer, Marilyn.** A Stick Is an Excellent Thing: Poems Celebrating Outdoor Play. 40 pp. Clarion 2012. ISBN 978-0-547-12493-3. Illustrated by LeUyen Pham.
Eighteen poems celebrate the old-fashioned kind of play, where the only equipment you need is a ball or a piece of chalk. Singer uses different styles of poetry and moves the poems from morning to dusk. Pham's illustrations match the retro feel of the games and feature a multicultural group of children, with wide eyes and wide smiles, enjoying the exciting play.
Poetry; Play

J
811

Singer, Marilyn. Follow Follow: A Book of Reverso Poems. 32 pp. Dial 2013. ISBN 978-0-8037-3769-3. Illustrated by Josée Masse. series.

As in *Mirror Mirror*, poems subvert traditional tales by offering two points of view on a story: what goes down on the left-hand of the page goes up on the right, with line breaks and punctuation revised for strategic effect. The twelve referenced tales include *Puss in Boots*, *The Little Mermaid*, and *The Twelve Dancing Princesses*, and acrylic illustrations mirror the poems' structures.
Poetry; Fairy tales; Folklore; Humorous poetry

J
811

Singer, Marilyn. Mirror Mirror: A Book of Reversible Verse. 32 pp. Dutton 2010. ISBN 978-0-525-47901-7. Illustrated by Josée Masse.
Through a poetic invention she dubs the *reverso*, Singer meditates on twelve fa-

miliar folktales, and, via the magic of shifting line breaks and punctuation, their shadows. Each free-verse poem has two stanzas, set on facing columns, where the second is the first reversed. Similarly bifurcated illustrations, Shrek-bright, face the cleverly constructed and insightful poems.

Poetry; Folklore; Fairy tales; Humorous poetry

Singer, Marilyn. Rutherford B., Who Was He?: Poems About Our Presidents. 56 pp. Hyperion 2013. ISBN 978-1-4231-7100-3. Illustrated by John Hendrix.

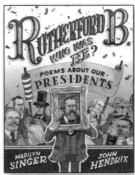

Forty-three presidents receive thirty-nine poems, touching on subjects such as political ideology, foreign policy, and domestic programs. A quote from George Washington in a bold hand-lettered font opens the book; in some cases, the richly colored art overwhelms the text. Brief biographical notes of each president give pertinent, but abbreviated, background information; sources are included.

Presidents—United States; History, American

Stevenson, Robert Louis. A Child's Garden of Verses. 80 pp. HarperCollins/Harper 2011. ISBN 978-0-06-028228-8. Illustrated by Barbara McClintock.

McClintock offers a complete edition of these old favorites in a format generous with white space and spot art as well as illustrative fantasies. Occasional full-page pictures set the scene; eponymous gardens burgeon invitingly throughout. McClintock's blend of old and new should attract readers. There's a table of contents, but no index.

Poetry

Vestergaard, Hope. Digger, Dozer, Dumper. 32 pp. Candlewick 2013. ISBN 978-0-7636-5078-0. Illustrated by David Slonim.

These playful verses sing the praises of sixteen trucks and the work they do. The lighthearted acrylic and charcoal illustrations enhance the poems' humor and give their subjects loads of personality. The same three children and friendly dog are pictured throughout, in drivers' seats and working alongside their truck friends. The book will make light work of even the toughest storytimes.

Poetry; Vehicles—Trucks

J
811

Wardlaw, Lee. Won Ton: A Cat Tale Told in Haiku. 40 pp. Holt 2011. ISBN 978-0-8050-8995-0. Illustrated by Eugene Yelchin.

In a series of haiku (technically "senryu"), a cat narrates the story of his adoption from a shelter and his new life. The animal's fear, pride, and gradual trust come across clearly in Wardlaw's poems. Yelchin's graphite and gouache pictures match the poems' sensitivity and humor, with the cat's wariness giving way over time to an enjoyment of his new environment.

Poetry; Animals—Cats; Poetry—Haiku

Wheeler, Lisa. Spinster Goose: Twisted Rhymes for Naughty Children. 48 pp. Atheneum (Simon & Schuster Children's Publishing) 2011. ISBN 978-1-4169-2541-5. Illustrated by Sophie Blackall.

Mother Goose's twisted sister stars in Wheeler's semi-subversive collection. The cautionary rhymes detail all manner of bad (cheating, bullying) or impolite behavior, made even funnier by a mock-formal typeface and decorously spacious pages. Blackall's ink and watercolor illustrations maintain a similar balance, with prim lines and sober colors displaying the mischief. A good first lesson in parody.

Poetry; Mother Goose; Humorous poetry

Worth, Valerie. Pug and Other Animal Poems. 40 pp. Farrar/Ferguson 2013. ISBN 978-0-374-35024-6. Illustrated by Steve Jenkins.

Like Jenkins's first collection of Worth's poems, *Animal Poems*, bold collages of precisely observed creatures dramatize eighteen welcome additions to Worth's oeuvre. The soulful "Pug" is a worried charmer ("Perhaps because, for / Dogs, they look / A lot like people"); a primeval black bull is "Rough-hewn, / From the planet's / Hard side, / From the cold / Black rock / That abides."

Poetry; Animals

Yolen, Jane and Dotlich, Rebecca Kai. Grumbles from the Forest: Fairy-Tale Voices with a Twist. 40 pp. Boyds/Wordsong 2013. ISBN 978-1-59078-867-7. Illustrated by Matt Mahurin.

Each of fifteen well-known fairy tales is distilled into two short poems, one written by Yolen, the other by Dotlich. The perspectives are mostly different and are often those of characters—or inanimate objects such as the princess's pea—not usually heard from in the traditional tales. Mahurin's varied, painterly illustrations help reinforce meaning of the occasionally oblique writing.

Poetry; Fairy tales

—FOCUS ON—
Odd Couples

Why Can't We Be Friends?

By Joy Fleishhacker

A former SLJ staffer, Joy Fleishhacker is a freelance writer and youth services librarian at Pikes Peak Library District in Colorado.

Filled with unlikely but enduring attachments, ostensibly incompatible Romeos and Juliets, and unexpected instances of true animal camaraderie, these books prove that affection can allow individuals to look beyond their differences and forge long-lasting bonds. The stories are entrancingly illustrated and skillfully told, ranging in tone from heartstring-tugging to funny-bone-tickling, and in style from fantastical to those based on fact. Appropriate for sharing aloud or reading independently, the stories target youngsters who are just beginning to explore social interactions independently, form friendships by choice, and realize that their actions can have positive or negative consequences. Many of these titles celebrate individuality while emphasizing the importance of finding common ground with others. They convey essential truths regarding the value of compromise, the emotionally empowering results of empathy, and the wonders of glimpsing the world through the eyes of another. The message that no one is ever truly alone echoes throughout the selections and provides inspiration and hope. Use these books to expand friendship storytimes or units; tease out overarching themes; and initiate discussions of tolerance, compassion, and community.

TALES OF THE HEART

Burks, James. Bird & Squirrel on the Run! illus. by author. Scholastic/Graphix. 2012. pap. $8.99. ISBN 978-0-545-31283-7.
  Gr 2-6–Stalked by a ferocious feline, two critters with polar-opposite personalities–carefree Bird and scared-of-everything Squirrel–flee together south toward safety,

and their hair-raising, humor-filled, save-each-other's-skin adventures gradually transform an uneasy alliance into deep-felt friendship. Burks's graphic novel sparkles with crisp color artwork, quip-cracking dialogue, and plenty of heart.

E
B

Buzzeo, Toni. One Cool Friend. illus. by David Small. Dial. 2012. RTE $16.99. ISBN 978-0-8037-3413-5.

PreS-Gr 3–A "very proper" tuxedo-wearing boy discovers a kindred spirit at the penguin display at the aquarium, pops the critter into his backpack, and goes about making Magellan feel at home, all under the large-size nose of his seemingly oblivious father. A hoot, with perfect comic interplay between the wryly straight-faced storytelling and supple-lined artwork.

E
C

Crummel, Susan Stevens & Dorothy Donohue. City Dog, Country Dog. illus. by Dorothy Donohue. Marshall Cavendish. 2004. RTE $16.95. ISBN 978-2-223-42222-7; pap. $7.99. ISBN 978-0-7614-5538-7.

K-Gr 4–After meeting at art school in France, best pals Henri T. Lapooch and Vincent van Dog must surmount discordant personalities and preferences to find common ground. Filled with clever references to the canine characters' true-life inspirations (Toulouse-Lautrec and van Gogh), this Aesop-based story blithely blends upbeat text, vibrant collage artwork, and a resounding moral ("Vive la difference!"). Audio version available from Spoken Arts Media.

J
Fic

Dicamillo, Kate & Alison McGhee. Bink & Gollie. illus. by Tony Fucile. Candlewick. 2010. RTE $15.99. ISBN 978-0-7636-3266-3; pap. $6.99. ISBN 978-0-7636-5954-7.

Gr 1-3–Two girls–one tiny, tousled, and puckish; the other tall, tidy, and coolly self-possessed; both delightfully quirky and headstrong–embark on three hilarious adventures that showcase their differences while celebrating the special bond they share. Droll dialogue, splattered-with-color cartoons, and perfect comic timing add up to a whole lot of fun. The zany escapades continue in *Bink & Gollie, Two for One* (Candlewick, 2012). DVD and audio version available from Weston Woods.

O

Esbaum, Jill. Tom's Tweet. illus. by Dan Santat. Knopf. 2011. Tr $16.99. ISBN 978-0-375-85171-1; PLB $19.99. ISBN 978-0-375-95171-8; ebook $8.99. ISBN 978-0-375-98472-3.

K-Gr 2–Coming across a fallen-out-of-the-nest baby bird, a scruffy stray cat exclaims, "Hello, breakfast," but "Dadburn it!," the quivering tot is just too skinny to consume, and "Consarn it!," too helpless to leave on its own. In this riotous read-aloud, rousing rhymes and rambunctious caricature-style cartoons describe how Tom goes from chompers-ready predator to tweety-cuddling chum.

Gorbachev, Valeri. How to Be Friends with a Dragon. illus. by author. Albert Whitman. 2012. Tr $16.99. ISBN 978-0-8075-3432-8.
PreS-Gr 2–Simon loves everything about dragons, and while listening to his older sister expound upon the basics of befriending these beasts (from "be nice" to wear your seatbelt if he takes you flying), the boy envisions imagination-soaring interactions with a smiling green-scaled companion. Engaging narrative and airy artwork gracefully balance realism with fantasy, humor with gentle affection.

Grey, Mini. The Adventures of the Dish and the Spoon. illus. by author. Knopf. 2006. Tr $16.95. ISBN 978-0-375-83691-6.
Gr 1-4–The nursery-rhyme twosome runs away to 1920s New York City, where they find fame as vaudeville stars, turn to crime after going broke, and are tragically separated after an unsuccessful heist. However, true love withstands the vagaries of fate, resulting in a joyful reunion years later. Colorful collages and snappy narrative shine with playful details and invigorating élan.

Howe, James. Otter and Odder: A Love Story. illus. by Chris Raschka. Candlewick. 2012. RTE $14. ISBN 978-0-7636-4174-0.
Gr 1-3–Gazing into the "round, sweet, glistening eyes" of his soon-to-be dinner, Otter finds himself falling for his food source, Myrtle the fish. Can this star-crossed, cross-species couple overcome wagging tongues and innate predator-prey instincts to find their happy-ever-after ending? The lyrical narrative and childlike artwork convey wise truths about following one's heart and cherishing love.

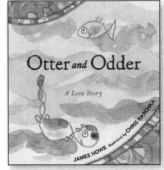

Kostecki-Shaw, Jenny Sue. Same, Same but Different. illus. by author. Holt/Christy Ottaviano. 2011. Tr $16.99. ISBN 978-0-8050-8946-2; ebook $9.99. ISBN 978-1-4668-1116-4.
K-Gr 2–When pen pals Elliot and Kailash begin to exchange drawings and letters, they discover that even though they live in two different countries–America and India–they have much in common. Jewel-toned mixed-media illustrations dynam-

ically depict details of both worlds, encouraging readers to identify aspects unique to each culture while appreciating the universality of shared interests and affection.

E
L
✱ *paperback*
Caldecott

Langstaff, John, retel. Frog Went A-Courtin'. illus by Feodor Rojankovsky. Harcourt. 1955. Tr $17. ISBN 978-0-15-230214-6; pap. $7. ISBN 978-0-15-633900-1. PreS-Gr 4–An amphibian dandy gallantly woos the lovely Mistress Mouse, wedding preparations are made, and the couple celebrates with animal and insect guests until a pouncing cat brings an end to the festivities and prompts an early honeymoon departure. This sprightly retelling of a folk song harmonizes toe-tapping couplets with spellbinding homespun artwork. Audio version available from Weston Woods.

Lear, Edward. The Owl and the Pussycat. illus. by Jan Brett. Putnam. 1991. Tr $17.99. ISBN 978-0-399-21925-2; pap. $6.99. ISBN 978-0-698-11367-1. PreS-Gr 4–Lear's whimsical poem about two seemingly mismatched lovers unfurls against a lush-hued, lavishly imagined Caribbean setting. Mingling detailed realism with fanciful charm, the sun-shimmering paintings depict the tender courtship between dashing fowl and dainty feline aboard their "pea-green boat," while another romance–a tale of two tropical fish separated and reunited–plays out beneath the ocean's surface.

Miller, Bobbi, retel. Miss Sally Ann and the Panther. illus. by Megan Lloyd. Holiday House. 2012. RTE $16.95. ISBN 978-0-8234-1833-6. K-Gr 3–When the feted American folk heroine meets a mean-as-tarnation varmint in the woods, a tree-felling, gorge-clawing, Milky Way-curdling brawl ensues, a "conbobberation" that lasts until both combatants prove their mettle, smile at one another, and become "great and glorious friends." A rip-roaring tall tale with tongue-tingling language and bold-as-brass artwork.

Pinkwater, Daniel. Bear in Love. illus. by Will Hillenbrand. Candlewick. 2012. RTE $15.99. ISBN 978-0-7636-4569-4. PreS–Someone has been leaving tasty treats for Bear, causing him to sing jubilant songs and to leave his own sweet offerings. Kindness adds to kindness until the two finally meet–it's a shy bunny–to share their mutual enthusiasm for food, music, and one another. This charmer soars with scrumptious storytelling and sweet-as-pie paintings.

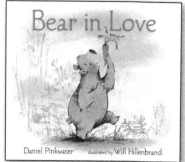

Daniel Pinkwater   illustrated by Will Hillenbrand

Richardson, Justin & Peter Parnell. And Tango Makes Three. illus. by Henry Cole. S & S. 2005. Tr $16.99. ISBN 978-0-6898-7845-9; ebook $12.99. ISBN 978-1-4424-2410-4.

PreS-Gr 3–Two male penguins forge an enduring bond, construct a nest, and start a family by caring for an abandoned egg. Set in New York City's Central Park Zoo and based on a true story, this tale pairs enchanting sherbet-hued watercolors and fine-tuned text to speak volumes about the importance of tolerance and the power of love.

Runton, Andy. Bright Lights and Starry Nights. illus. by author. (Owly & Wormy Series). S & S/Atheneum. 2012. Tr $15.99. ISBN 978-1-4169-5775-1; ebook $12.99. ISBN 978-1-4424-5439-2.

K-Gr 3–Two unlikely besties embark on a star-gazing camping trip marked by mishaps that test their verve and their nerve before finally catching sight of an awe-inspiring vista and winning a few new pals. Starring an amiable round-eyed owl and a spunky comma-shaped worm, this wordless sequel to *Friends All Aflutter!* (Atheneum, 2011) conveys events and emotions with ebullient drenched-in-dusky-hues cartoons and pictograph thought bubbles.

Sauer, Tammi. Nugget & Fang: Friends Forever or Snack Time? illus. by Michael Slack. Houghton Harcourt. Apr. 2013. Tr $16.99. ISBN 978-0-547-85285-0.

PreS-Gr 2–Nugget and Fang are boon companions until Nugget swims off to school and is taught that minnows can't be buddies with sharks (as per the food chain). They part ways, but when Nugget's life is endangered, faithful Fang gets the chance to prove his affection. Tongue-in-gill text and buoyant deep-water-hued cartoons send a heartfelt message about friendship.

Stead, Philip C. A Home for Bird. illus. by author. Roaring Brook/Neal Porter. 2012. Tr $16.99. ISBN 978-1-59643-711-1.

PreS-Gr 4–While out foraging for "interesting things," a toad instead finds a friend (an illustration shows the wooden-looking bird falling off a cuckoo clock on a passing-by pickup). Worried that his pal's stony silence is symptomatic of homesickness, Vernon takes Bird on a daring quest to locate his abode. Deadpan text and effervescent artwork relate a smile-inducing tale of altruism and empathy. Audio version available from Recorded Books.

E
S ♀

paperback

Steig, William. Amos & Boris. illus. by author. Farrar. 1971. Tr $17.99. ISBN 978-0-374-30227-6; pap. $7.99. ISBN 978-0-312-53566-7.

K-Gr 5–While sailing the high seas, a venturesome mouse falls overboard and is rescued by an affable whale. Despite vast disparities in size and stomping grounds, the two mammals forge a friendship that resurfaces years later when Boris ends up in dire need of Amos's assistance. Lighthearted watercolors and an eloquent narrative create a wise, witty, and wonder-filled tale.

O

Weeks, Sarah. Woof: A Love Story. illus. by Holly Berry. HarperCollins/Laura Geringer. 2009. Tr $16.99. ISBN 978-0-06-025007-2.

K-Gr 2–Smitten by a pretty white cat with sparkling green eyes, a dog tries to articulate his feelings to her, but his "woofs" and "grrrs" only send her scampering up a tree…until he digs up a "shiny brass [trom]bone," trumpets his emotions with passionate gusto, and wins her heart. A read-aloud romp with breezy rhymes and exuberant collage artwork.

E
W

Willems, Mo. City Dog, Country Frog. illus. by Jon J. Muth. Hyperion/Disney. 2010. RTE $17.99. ISBN 978-1-4231-0300-4.

PreS-Gr 2–On a glorious spring day, a tail-wagging pooch meets a smiling amphibian and amity blossoms. Through the seasons, City Dog returns to frolic and reminisce with his pal. When winter's visit finds Country Frog no longer there, spring's return brings the comfort of remembrance and a new companion. Spare text and touched-with-light watercolors create an uplifting ode to friendship.

EASY READERS, ENDEARING FRIENDSHIPS

O

Bell, Cece. Rabbit & Robot: The Sleepover. illus. by author. Candlewick. 2012. Tr $14.99. ISBN 978-0-7636-5475-7.

K-Gr 2–When the evening doesn't go as planned, single-minded Rabbit overreacts, but logical Robot remains unruffled and demonstrates how to roll with the punches, until he runs out of steam and Rabbit comes to the rescue. Funny situations, nuts-and-bolts visual high jinx, and a satisfying meeting-of-minds resolution leave readers rolling with laughter.

O

Howe, James. Houndsley and Catina: Plink and Plunk. illus. by Marie-Louise Gay. Candlewick. 2009. Tr $15.99. ISBN 978-0-7636-3385-1; pap. $3.99. ISBN 978-0-7636-6640-8.

K-Gr 2–Though best friends, a floppy-eared dog and snowy-furred cat have dissimilar interests–he likes canoeing while she likes bicycling. After a few frustrating outings, they discover that they must help one another overcome fears in order to share these favorite pastimes. Part of a charmingly illustrated and invitingly told series featuring two winsome characters.

Lobel, Arnold. Frog and Toad Are Friends. illus. by author. HarperCollins. 1970. Tr $16.99. ISBN 978-0-06-023957-2; pap. $3.99. ISBN 978-0-06-444020-2; eb-ook $4.99. ISBN 978-0-06-197410-6.

K-Gr 3–Frog is outgoing and spontaneous while Toad is more staid and set in his ways, but these companions share a tried-and-true friendship filled with heart-warming empathy and a genuine appreciation for one another's foibles and forti-tudes. The first in a series of grin-making adventures, told with accessible language, packed-with-personality artwork, and everlasting child appeal. Audio version avail-able from HarperFestival.

Weeks, Sarah. Mac and Cheese and the Perfect Plan. illus. by Jane Manning. Harp-erCollins. 2012. Tr $16.99. ISBN 978-0-06-117082-9; pap. $3.99. ISBN 987-0-06-117084-3.

K-Gr 2–In this second adventure about two feline friends, happy-go-lucky Mac is determined to get curmudgeonly Cheese out of the alley and off to the seashore, but when Cheese's hemming and hawing causes them to miss the bus, he grudgingly finds a way to placate Mac and make some fun. Rhyme-filled text and comical art-work shine with humor and affection.

Willems, Mo. Let's Go for a Drive! illus. by author. (Elephant and Piggie Series). Hy-perion. 2012. RTE $8.99. ISBN 978-142316482-1.

K-Gr 2–Meticulous-minded Gerald the elephant formulates a plan for the per-fect road trip, sending ever-peppy Piggie scrambling to gather supplies. When one small detail (they don't have a car) derails the undertaking—as well as Gerald–Pig-gie cheerfully comes up with a new plan. Kinetic cartoons, zesty text, and an unfor-gettable friendship combine in this laugh-out-loud addition to a never-miss series.

TRUE TALES

Buckley, Carol. Tarra & Bella: The Elephant and Dog Who Became Best Friends. photos by author. Putnam. 2009. RTE $16.99. ISBN 978-0-399-25443-7.

K-Gr 5–After years in the entertainment industry, Tarra retired to Tennessee's El-ephant Sanctuary but never paired off with a pachyderm pal like the other inhabitants. Surprisingly, the role of BFF was filled by a feisty stray dog. Crystal-clear photos and straightforward text describe how the two unlikely but devoted companions romp and play, communicate, and look after one another.

J
599.63

Hatkoff, Isabella, Craig Hatkoff, & Paula Kahumbu. Owen & Mzee: The True Story of a Remarkable Friendship. photos by Peter Greste. Scholastic. 2006. Tr $16.99. ISBN 978-0-439-82973-1.

K-Gr 5–Stranded on a coral reef by a 2004 tsunami, a baby hippopotamus was rescued, transported to an animal sanctuary in Kenya, and placed in an enclosure occupied by a 130-year-old tortoise. The long-lasting bond that ensued has amazed scientists and inspired many. Engaging close-up images and compelling text relate events with clarity and an emphasis on hope. The story continues in *Owen & Mzee: The Language of Friendship* (Scholastic, 2007).

Jurmain, Susan Tripp. Worst of Friends: Thomas Jefferson, John Adams, and the True Story of an American Feud. illus. by Larry Day. Dutton. 2011. Tr $16.99. ISBN 978-0-525-47903-1.

Gr 2-5–As different as "pickles and ice cream," tall, shy Thomas and short, loquacious John were the best of friends, working together to shape their newly born nation, until a passionate disagreement about presidential powers caused a political and personal rift that only time–and true affection–could overcome. Vivacious text and witty pencil-and-watercolor artwork blend historical detail with winning humor. Audio version available from Recorded Books.

E
L

Larson, Kirby & Mary Nethery. Two Bobbies: A True Story of Hurricane Katrina, Friendship, and Survival. illus. by Jean Cassels. Walker. 2008. Tr $16.99. ISBN 978-0-8027-9754-4; PLB $17.89. ISBN 978-0-8027-9755-1.

K-Gr 3–Left homeless by the devastating storm, a dog and a cat–dubbed Bobbi and Bob Cat for their bobbed tails–wandered the streets of New Orleans for months, surviving only by sticking together, until they were finally rescued by animal shelter volunteers. Simple narrative and soft-toned realistic paintings tell a stirring tale of companionship. DVD available from Nutmeg Media.

Thimmesh, Catherine. Friends. Houghton Harcourt. 2011. Tr $16.99. ISBN 978-0-547-39010-9; ebook $16.99. ISBN 978-0-547-76921-9.

K-Gr 2–Strikingly photographed instances of remarkable animal amity–an elderly orangutan cuddling with a cat, a lion cub and piglet snuggled up and snoozing, a polar bear romping with a sled dog–are paired with simple rhyming verses that elucidate the wonders of friendship (prose paragraphs provide background information). This audience-grabber will inspire discussion along with "oohs" and "awws."

ON THE WEB

For Teachers:

ePALS: Global Community. www.epals.com. ePals Corporation. Herndon, VA. (Accessed 6/19/14).
Connecting educators, students, and parents in approximately 200 countries, this social learning network for teacher-designed interactions includes monitored email exchanges, collaborative projects with partner classrooms, student forums, and globe-spanning book discussion activities. Easy to use, with embedded translation, useful search tools, student-tracking options, and abundant educator resources.

Friendship Through Education. www.friendshsiptrougheducation.org. Friendship Through Education Consortium. (Accessed 6/19/14).
Dedicated to building a culture of peace by facilitating online and offline interactions among youngsters worldwide, this site provides a clearinghouse of communication-fostering opportunities (letter/email exchanges, global projects, etc.). Though the home page is outdated, the links and resources will be useful to teachers looking to expand classroom horizons.

For Students:

Animal Odd Couples. www.pbs.org/wnet/nature/episodes/animal-odd-couples/full-episode/8009. PBS/Nature. (Accessed 6/19/14).
Gr 3 Up–Featuring a variety of amazing cross-species relationships, this captivating documentary blends stunning photography with insightful narration from caregivers and scientists to explore why animals form these specials bonds. Premiered on November 7, 2012, the episode can be viewed in its entirety or sampled through shorter topic-specific chapters.

Owen & Mzee. www.owenandmzee.com. Turtle Pond Publications. New York, NY. (Accessed 6/19/14).
K-Gr 5–Well-designed and child-friendly, this site blends text, photos, and video to provide background about the two famed pals and their home at Kenya's Haller Park. From a sing-along, to a videomaker, to a sprinkled-with-Swahili-words story section, the activities and games are inviting, entertaining, and informative.

Unlikely Animal Friends. channel.nationalgeographic.com/wild/unlikely-animal-friends. National Geographic. (Accessed 6/19/14).
K-Gr 5–Brief, easy-to-browse video clips from the TV series introduce an array of unusual duos, including a Great Dane who mothers an orphaned fawn, a young baboon who cavorts with a bush baby, and a long-lasting relationship between a stray cat and a bear. Elucidating and adorable viewing.

- -

—FOCUS ON—

A Writer's Tools

Wordcraft

By Barbara Wysocki

Barbara Wysocki recently retired from the position of co-director of Children's Services at the Cora J. Belden Library in Rocky Hill, CT.

- -

*"Indeed, learning to write may be a part of learning to read. For all I know, writing comes out of a superior devotion to reading." —*Eudora Welty

It's unlikely that Ms. Welty was talking about a first grader putting words on paper, but the connection between reading and writing is a foundation in education. "Writing helps a student think," says Assistant Superintendent Heather Sheridan-Thomas of TST (Tompkins-Seneca-Tioga) BOCES district in Central New York. "They slow down enough to locate thoughts they already have, process new information they are learning, and critically evaluate information and ideas."

Once upon a time writing meant studying penmanship charts and using ink pots. Higher-level thinking included diagramming sentences. Today's nimble-fingered keyboard experts are often proficient at texting and typing before they finish the primary grades. Now the emphasis is on self-expression and analysis, but communicating effectively also includes grammar, punctuation, and parts of speech. Keren Taylor, Executive Director of WriteGirl, a California nonprofit promoting creativity and self-expression to empower girls, says, "Writing is a core competency for virtually any academic subject."

Crafting written work is a two-part invention. Questions such as who, when, what, where, why, and how are melded with heart plus mind for results potentially life-altering and -affirming. While we accentuate practical books here, there's also a section intended to inspire. Add these titles to your pencil and paper toolbox so students can build writing proficiency.

NAME ME A NOUN, VISIT ME WITH A VERB

Byers, Patricia. One Sheep, Two Sheep: A Book of Collective Nouns. illus. by Tamsin Ainslie. Little Hare. 2011. Tr $10.99. ISBN 978-1-921541-45-2.

K-Gr 2–Children wearing matching dress-up outfits introduce a gaggle of geese, a knot of frogs, a kaleidoscope of butterflies, and six more animal groups that explore the concept and vocabulary when nouns multiply. Pastel illustrations offer a playful way to start students' search for expanded word choices.

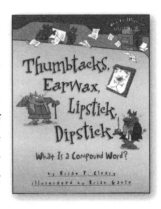

Cleary, Brian P. Thumbtacks, Earwax, Lipstick, Dipstick: What Is a Compound Word? illus. by Brian Gable. (Words Are CATegorical® Series.) Lerner. 2011. RTE $16.95. ISBN 978-0-7613-4917-4.

Gr 2-4–In this latest addition to the eye-catching, feline-filled cartoon series, comical pictures and brief text demonstrate that compound words come in many forms and lengths. Cleary concludes with a reminder that though these words are often longer, decoding them is easily done by taking them apart.

Coffelt, Nancy. Big, Bigger, Biggest! illus. by author. Holt. 2009. RTE $16.95. ISBN 978-0-8050-8089-6.

K-Gr 2–Broad sweeps of bold color make 21 animals the perfect menagerie to show comparatives and superlatives for size, speed, hunger, and tiredness. Descriptive adjectives, such as "humongous," "gooey," and "wee," modify noun synonyms to enrich a simple, yet effective way to encourage writing vocabulary.

☐ **Rayevsky, Kim.** Antonyms, Synonyms, and Homonyms. illus. by Robert Rayevsky. Holiday 428. House. 2006. RTE $16.95. ISBN 978-0-8234-1889-3.

Gr 1-4–A spaceship swoops in on the opening endpapers, and readers follow a cartoonish, ball-capped alien experiencing the three title word types on mixed-media spreads. "Up" a mountain, then "down" into the ocean he goes. At the end of each bustling word adventure, additional jam-packed pages offer more examples.

☐ **Traynor, Tracy.** Cheese Please, Chimpanzees: Fun with Spelling. illus. by Lily Bronfeyn. Milet. 2008. pap. $6.95. ISBN 978-1-84059-511-6.

PreS-Gr 2–More than a clever rhyming book, this slim volume strings together multiple ways to spell one sound, for example, "I" "spy" "bow-tie" and "high" in a single sentence. Vivid spreads illustrate sometimes amusing images. The book concludes with 11 new same-sound lists ready for a class project.

THE POWER OF POSITIVE PUNCTUATION

☐ **Bruno, Elsa Knight.** Punctuation Celebration. illus. by Jenny Whitehead. Holt. 2009. RTE $17.95. ISBN 978-08050-7973-9.

Gr 1-4–Some of the rhymes in ·the dozen poems are a stretch, but the zany detailed art makes everything fresh. With concepts kept simple and choices wisely limited, this is a good resource for introducing the subject. The field day theme is likely to draw interest, and the spreads give written examples backed by pictures.

☐ **Budzik, Mary.** Punctuation: The Write Stuff! illus. by Simon Basher. Kingfisher. 2010. pap. $7.99. ISBN 978-0-7534-6420-5.

Gr 3-8–After opening with information on sentences and capital letters, cartoon characters represent commas, colons, apostrophes, and other punctuation marks. Perky, first-person characterizations ("Straight up and down, I'm the party-hearty punctuation mark") combine with clear examples ("You're the best!") to form an effective and friendly guide. An enclosed poster adds visual cues for student follow-up.

☐ **Pulver, Robin.** Punctuation Takes a Vacation. illus. by Lynn Rowe Reed. Holiday House. 2003. RTE $17.95. ISBN 978-0-8234-1687-5; pap. $7.95. ISBN 978-0-8234-1820-6.

K-Gr 3–After days of punctuation instruction, featured in bright paintings, a class takes a rest and so do all the punctuation marks. While clever postcards arrive from quotations and other characters out at Take-a-Break Lake, Mr. Wright's kids are lost without their grammatical guides. More introductory than instructional, this is a fun way to open discussion. Audio version available from Live Oak Media.

J
+28.2

Truss, Lynne. The Girl's Like Spaghetti: Why, You Can't Manage Without Apostrophes! illus. by Bonnie Timmons. Putnam. 2007. RTE $16.99. ISBN 978-0-399-24706-4.

Gr 2–5–Do the family pets like your father, or does your canine act like him? It's all in the apostrophe, as in "The dogs like my dad" or "The dog's like my dad." Comical watercolor cartoons are set on opposite pages to show punctuation-sensitive sentence pairs, all dependent on the apostrophe for meaning.

SEEMS LIKE A SIMILE, MIGHT BE A METAPHOR

Brennan-Nelson, Denise. My Daddy Likes to Say. illus. by Jane Monroe Donovan. Sleeping Bear. 2009. Tr $15.95. ISBN 978-158536-432-9.
K-Gr 3–Common fatherly conversational gambits, such as "You're driving me up the wall" and "You're coming out of your shell," are among the many idioms woven into 13 poems, complete with brief explanations and the backgrounds of familiar phrases. The spreads feature soft, sometimes silly, visual interpretations of the poetry.

Leedy, Loreen & Pat Street. There's a Frog in My Throat!: 440 Animal Sayings a Little Bird Told Me. illus. by Loreen Leedy. Holiday House. 2003. RTE $18.95. ISBN 978-0-8234-1774-2; pap. $8.95. ISBN 978-0-8234-1819-0.

Gr 2–5–More fun than a barrel of monkeys, this lively collection of similes, metaphors, idioms, and proverbs goes from the backyard and farmyard to jungles and seas with traditional and new creature sayings. Brief explanations and appealing illustrations expand each phrase. Silly and serious, it's all teachable fun.

Paul, Ann Whitford. Word Builder. illus. by Kurt Cyrus. S & S. 2009. RTE $16.99. ISBN 978-1-4169-3981-8.
K-Gr 4–Using a construction site complete with heavy equipment set on bold spreads, this large-scale picture book is a visual and verbal metaphor as letters com-

bine to make words and words are arranged into sentences. Paragraphs grow from there until they turn into chapters. A great way to attract reluctant boys to writing, but so visually stirring it has broad appeal.

INSPIRATION MEETS PERSPIRATION

Agee, Jon. Mr. Putney's Quacking Dog. illus. by author. Scholastic. 2010. RTE $16.95. ISBN 978-0-545-16203-6.

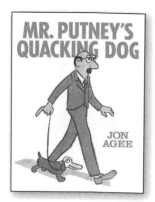

K-Gr 4–Readers follow a seriously silly, mustachioed man through his everyday, yet ridiculous, encounters as he wakes with an "alarmadillo," is sheltered poorly by a "giroof," lunches with a "slobster," and hangs around 17 more play-on-words creatures. This soft-toned picture book has turn-the-page surprises so students can guess or try to make their own amazing animals.

Boucher, Françoize. I Love Words. illus. by author. Kane/Miller. 2010. pap. $14.99. ISBN 978-1-935279-48-8.

Gr 2-5–Designed as an individual activity book, this oversize paperback doubles as a source for classroom wordplay with riddles and secret codes. Simple two-color line drawings and hand-written text have the feel of a child's personal effort, but the charts are easily adapted for board work. Helpful for quick fill-in lessons.

Curry, Don L. Willie's Word World. illus. by Rick Stromoski. (Rookie Reader Skill Set Series). Children's Press. 2005. pap. $4.95. ISBN 978-0-516-25288-9.

K-Gr 2–Use this easy reader as a lesson model as it presents a classroom exercise in simple, alliterative sentences such as, "'Little Lucy licks lizard lollipops,' Lincoln said." Each double-page illustration includes a cartoonish balloon picturing the alliteration. Older classes could devise whole books in this style using more sophisticated vocabulary.

Kostecki-Shaw, Jenny Sue. Same, Same but Different. illus. by author. Holt. 2011. RTE $16.99. ISBN 978-0-8050-8946-2.

K-Gr 2–Cheerful pictures and written notes pass between two boys, Elliot in the U.S. and Kailash in India, as they describe their lives. Though many of the details are unique to their own situation, the boys find connections that span their continents and experiences. A great introduction to the concept of pen pals.

Pulver, Robin. Thank You, Miss Doover. illus. by Stephanie Roth Sisson. Holiday House. 2010. RTE $16.95. ISBN 978-0-8234-2046-9.

Gr 1-3–When Miss Doover begins the lesson on thank-you notes, Jack is confident he can write one to his Great Aunt Gertie very quickly. But his teacher shepherds him through several changes until he sees how to communicate appreciation clearly. Lively spreads are populated with helpful word balloons and thank-you note revisions.

Seskin, Steve. Sing My Song: A Kid's Guide to Songwriting. w/CD. illus. by Eve Aldridge, et al. Tricycle. 2008. Tr $18.99. ISBN 978-1-5824-6266-0.

Gr 3-7–A dozen class-written songs with brightly diverse, facing illustrations demonstrate the words for the musical projects undertaken when Seskin worked with elementary-school students. The results can be heard on the accompanying CD, which also provides melodies and ideas for teachers.

ON THE WEB

For Teachers

Writing with Writers. teacher.scholastic.com/writewit. Scholastic. (Accessed 6/19/14).

Familiar authors present nine step-by-step genre workshops, including biography, myth, news, and poetry, accompanied by lesson plans. Elementary and middle grade students can work independently, or teachers can utilize assessment and rubric information for classroom projects.

For Students

The Story Kitchen. brucevanpatter.com/storykitchen.html. Bruce Van Patter (Accessed 6/19/14).

Gr 2-5–Devised by a cartoonist/author, this site encourages users to choose from a brief list of heroes, places, and villains to jumpstart their writing. For budding writers who need more support, printable "story starters" with open endings are provided.

Word Central. wordcentral.com. Merriam-Webster, Inc. (Accessed 6/19/14).

Gr 3 Up–Students can search the dictionary, thesaurus, and rhyming resources or enjoy interactive features that include word jumbles and interactive games that build vocabulary. Includes unobtrusive ads for Merriam-Webster products.

MEDIA PICKS

By Phyllis Levy Mandell

Writing for Children (Series). 5 DVDs. 23 min. ea. with tchr's. guide. Prod. by Schlessing-
er Media. Dist. by Library Video Co. (libraryvideo.com). 2004. $74.88 ser., $14.95
ea. Includes: Expository Writing (ISBN 1-57225-919-1); Story Writing (ISBN
1-57225-20-5); Types of Writing (ISBN 1-57225-921-3); The Writing Process
(ISBN 1-57225-922-1); Writing Resources (ISBN 1-57225-923-X).

K-Gr 4–Four children who make up the staff of the magazine *Wordswork* and their
publisher, Professor Plot, explore the writing process as they publish each issue.
Each program, narrated by the children, examines a different aspect of writing.
There are fun segments, such as a show called "The Organizers" featuring a detective, and an over-the-top talk-show spoof.

Eds. note: The full version of "Wordcraft" can be found online at http://ow.ly/yiiHD.

Religion

Adler, David A. The Story of Hanukkah. 32 pp. Holiday 2011. ISBN 978-0-8234-
2295-1. Illustrated by Jill Weber.

Adler's straightforward, accessible retelling of the Hanukkah story details King Antio-
chus IV's coronation, his oppression of Jews, and triumphant revolt by the Maccabees.
The narrative concludes with modern-day observances of events; a recipe for latkes
and instructions for the dreidel game are appended. Acrylic illustrations richly accented with deep blues and luminous golds recall ancient friezes and ceramics.
Religious Holidays; Holidays—Hanukkah; Jews; Religion—Judaism

J
394.2 **Farmer, Jacqueline.** O Christmas Tree: Its History and Holiday Traditions. 32 pp. Charlesbridge 2010. ISBN 978-1-58089-238-4. PE ISBN 978-1-58089-239-1.

Illustrated by Joanne Friar. From the evergreen boughs used by ancient Egyptians
to celebrate the winter solstice to modern LED lights and pink aluminum trees,
Farmer provides a wealth of information about the social history of the Christmas
tree. She also traces its development both as plant and as cash crop. Illustrated with

warm, cheerful gouache pictures, the book is accessible and well organized.
Customs and Holidays; Holidays—Christmas; Trees; Christmas trees

King James Bible. Christmas Is Here. 32 pp. Simon (Simon & Schuster Children's Publishing) 2010. ISBN 978-1-4424-0822-7. Illustrated by Lauren Castillo.
Over three wordless spreads, a child walks with his family to see a live Nativity scene. The boy looks thoughtfully into the manger at a sleeping Christ child, and readers are transported to the first Christmas. The seemingly incongruous pairing—formal Bible verses and Castillo's child-friendly illustrations—works beautifully, with subdued colors and unfussy compositions making the archaic text more accessible.
Religious Holidays; Religion—Nativity; Holidays—Christmas; Religion—Bible; Religion—Jesus Christ

Mackall, Dandi Daley. Listen to the Silent Night. 32 pp. Dutton 2011. ISBN 978-0-525-42276-1. Illustrated by Steve Johnson.
This narrative poem relates the Nativity through its sounds: the *flip, flap, flap* of Joseph's sandals; the *flut-flut-flutter* of descending angels. Mackall's carefully constructed verse emphasizes that while the first Christmas may not have been a "silent night," it was a "miraculous" one. Peaceful illustrations eloquently capture the range of emotions from Mary's weariness to the joy of Jesus' birth.
Religious Holidays; Religion—Christianity; Religion—Nativity; Holidays—Christmas; Religion—Jesus Christ; Sound

Summers, Susan. The Greatest Gift: The Story of the Other Wise Man. 32 pp. Barefoot 2011. ISBN 978-1-84686-578-7. Illustrated by Jackie Morris.
When Artaban stops to heal a man, he's left behind by the three other Magi. After years of helping the distressed, Artaban arrives in Jerusalem just as Jesus is about to be crucified. He's faced with one final dilemma: try to free Jesus or release a girl from captivity. The heartwarming story, told with appropriately formal language, is accompanied by rich, saturated watercolors.
Religious Holidays; Holidays—Christmas; Religion—Nativity; Religion—Jesus Christ; Religion—Christianity; Behavior—Kindness

Wolf, Gita. The Enduring Ark. 20 pp. Tara 2013. ISBN 978-93-80340-18-0. Illustrated by Joydeb Chitrakar.
An accordion-style pictorial narration of the Flood unfolds to a nine-foot spread of Noah and his wife gathering creatures; the reverse side follows the Ark to its landing.

Wolf's well-phrased account—an Indian version of the story common to many cultures—is generally straightforward, a fine complement to Chitrakar's striking art in the Bengal Patua style of scroll painting.

General Religion; Religion—Noah (Bible); India

- -

—FOCUS ON—

Celebrations and Festivals

A Calendar of Holidays

By Heidi R. Estrin

Heidi R. Estrin is Library Director at the Feldman Children's Library,
Congregation B'nai Israel of Boca Raton, FL.

- -

Kids love holidays. Any kind of celebration or festival brings a break in routine, an excuse for a party, perhaps a chance to dress up. Multigenerational family gatherings and the enacting of annual rituals bring a sense of continuity, and sharing celebrations with the greater community enhances a sense of belonging. Whether the festivities are based on personal rites of passage, religious traditions, or historical events, the key is togetherness. Celebrating together strengthens the bonds among people and reaffirms our identities, individually and collectively.

The books featured here have been arranged to follow the course of a year. You'll notice that Christmas and Hanukkah are missing; they are covered annually in *School Library Journal's* October issue. Those familiar with National Geographic's beautiful "Holidays Around the World" series of photo-essays may also wonder at its exclusion. Rather than list the individual titles, I am making a blanket recommendation for these finely crafted books on Chinese New Year, Valentine's Day, Easter, Passover, Cinco de Mayo, Independence Day, Rosh Hashanah and Yom Kippur, Halloween, Thanksgiving, Ramadan and Eid al-Fitr, Hanukkah, Diwali, Kwanzaa, and Christmas. Each title combines crisp international photography with broad holiday themes and descriptions of specific customs.

The titles annotated here are mostly short, lively, illustrated books aimed at younger readers. They represent a mix of realistic fiction, nonfiction guides to history and observance, and a few imaginative tales of anthropomorphic animals and objects. Consider reading them aloud to enhance the celebrations of the holidays described.

LATE WINTER TO SPRING

Compestine, Ying Chang. The Runaway Wok: A Chinese New Year Tale. illus. by Sebastià Serra. Dutton. 2011. RTE $16.99. ISBN 978-0-525-42068-2.

K-Gr 4–This Chinese twist on a Danish folktale introduces a helpful wok that takes from the rich and gives to the poor, bringing rice, toys, and money so the community can celebrate the New Year. Lively acrylic paintings and a satisfyingly repetitive text showcase Chinese New Year customs.

Flanagan, Alice K. Carnival. illus. by Roberta Collier-Morales. (Holidays and Festivals Series). Compass Point. 2003. PLB $25.32. ISBN 978-0-756-50478-6.
K-Gr 4–This basic but thorough introduction pays special attention to Mardi Gras as celebrated in New Orleans, but the holiday's variants in Brazil, the Caribbean, Canada, and Mexico are also discussed. Complemented by festive drawings.

Tompert, Ann. Saint Valentine. illus. by Kestutis Kasparavicius. Boyds Mills. 2004. RTE $15.95. ISBN 978-1-590-78181-4.
Gr 2-5–History and legend seamlessly combine in this picture-book biography of a Christian priest persecuted for his beliefs in third-century Rome. Connections with the modern holiday include Valentine's sending parchment hearts to imprisoned Christians, performing secret marriage ceremonies, and his February 14th martyrdom. Gentle watercolors set the scene.

Rockwell, Anne. St. Patrick's Day. illus. by Lizzy Rockwell. HarperCollins. 2010. Tr $14.99. ISBN 978-0-06-050197-6.
PreS-Gr 2–Mrs. Madoff's students learn about St. Patrick's Day and Ireland by writing reports, playacting, and dancing in this gentle, cheerfully illustrated story. The

well-known mother-daughter duo offer similarly satisfying fare in *Thanksgiving Day* (HarperCollins, 1999).

E
Holiday
Wallace, Nancy Elizabeth. The Valentine Express. illus. by the author. Marshall Caven-dish. 2004. Tr $16.95. ISBN 978-0-761-45183-9.
PreS-Gr 2–Wallace's signature papercut bunnies learn about the history and customs of Valentine's Day at school, then go home and spread the love by making heart-themed gifts for their neighbors. Instructions for the charming crafts are incorporated into this upbeat story.

Wong, Janet S. This Next New Year. illus. by Yangsook Choi. Farrar. 2000. Tr $16.99. ISBN 978-0-374-35503-6.
PreS-Gr 2–A young Korean-Chinese protagonist, along with his French-German and Hopi-Mexican friends, prepares for the annual lunar celebration of renewal by cleaning his home and his body, eating special foods, and vowing to think positively. Bright illustrations and rhythmic text depict both the universal and the culture-specific traditions associated with the start of a new year.

SPRING TO SUMMER

Ada, Alma Flor. Let Me Help!/¡Quiero ayudar! illus. by Angela Domínguez. Children's Book Press. 2010. RTE $16.95. ISBN 978-0-89239-232-2.

Gr 2-5–Perico the parrot echoes young Martita: "Let me help! Let me help!" as the family makes tamales and paper flowers for Cinco de Mayo, but his offer is rejected. Yet when a bridge knocks the top off the family's decorated barge, Perico helps at last, redecorating by perching aloft, colorful wings spread. Bilingual text and bright paintings create a festive atmosphere.

E
Holiday
Brett, Jan. The Easter Egg. illus. by author. Putnam. 2010. RTE $17.99 ISBN 978-0-399-25238-9.
K-Gr 2–Bunnies decorate eggs, hoping to be named the Easter Bunny's helper. Hoppi is distracted from the competition when a robin's egg falls from its nest, but his valiant caregiving pays off. Delicate and detailed, the richly hued illustrations evoke the beauty of this springtime holiday.

E

Holiday

Cox, Judy. Cinco de Mouse-O! illus. by Jeffrey Ebbeler. Holiday House. 2010. Tr $16.95. ISBN 978-0-8234-2194-7.

K-Gr 2–Mouse finds traditional foods and mariachi music at a Cinco de Mayo festival. Bright, dynamic illustrations show him perching on a musician's sombrero, riding the burro piñata, and avoiding the predatory Cat. An introduction provides history, while the entertaining story supplies a survey of the holiday's activities. For an equally enticing adventure involving these engaging rivals, try *One Is a Feast for Mouse: A Thanksgiving Tale* (Holiday House, 2008).

E

D

Demunn, Michael. The Earth Is Good: A Chant in Praise of Nature. illus. by Jim McMullan. Scholastic. 1999. RTE $15.95. ISBN 978-0-590-35010-5.

PreS-Gr 2–While Earth Day isn't mentioned by name, this book embodies its spirit. Simple, powerful statements, "The sun is good./The earth is good./The trees are good," are accompanied by lush watercolors of a joyful boy and his dog immersing themselves in nature. The final statement, "And you are good," helps readers see themselves as stewards of the Earth.

O

Hanft, Josh. The Miracles of Passover. illus. by Seymour Chwast. Blue Apple. 2007. Tr $15.95. ISBN 978-1-59354-600-7.

K-Gr 3–Liftable flaps and bright cartoon-style illustrations enhance this simple retelling of the biblical Exodus. Readers will learn about the Passover Seder and the story it recalls of Moses and Pharaoh and the Jewish slaves' escape from ancient Egypt. An engaging account, relayed with a clever, interactive design.

O

Kahn, Hena. Night of the Moon: A Muslim Holiday Story. illus. by Julie Paschkis. Chronicle. 2008. Tr $16.99. ISBN 978-0-8118-6062-8.

Gr 2-4–A Pakistani-American girl celebrates the lunar Muslim holidays, Ramadan and Eid-al-Fitr. Her family participates in holiday customs, fasting by day and eating special foods at night, sharing food with the poor, visiting a mosque, and painting hands with henna. Intricate, deeply colored illustrations portray a diverse Muslim-American community.

J

394.2

Lehman-Wilzig, Tami. Passover Around the World. illus. by Elizabeth Wolf. Kar-Ben. 2006. RTE $15.95. ISBN 978-1-58013-213-8; pap. $7.95. ISBN 978-1-58013-215-2.

Gr 2-5–Universal and particular customs of the Jewish holiday are explored with a focus on the United States, Gibraltar, Turkey, Ethiopia, India, Iran, Morocco, and

Israel. Quick facts, maps, recipes, and stories of contemporary celebrations in each country are accompanied by warm paintings. A fun, international approach. See also *Hanukkah Around the World* (Lerner, 2009).

○ **Osborne, Mary Pope.** Happy Birthday, America: A Story of Independence Day. illus. by Peter Catalanotto. Millbrook/Roaring Brook. 2003. Tr $15.95 978-0-7613-1675-6; PLB $22.90. ISBN 978-0-7613-2761-5; pap. $6.95. ISBN 978-1-59643-051-8.
K-Gr 2–An extended family enjoys a small-town celebration with a carnival, parade, concert, public reading of the Declaration of Independence, and fireworks. Nostalgic watercolors evoke the warmth of the community. An author's note explains the origin of the holiday.

○ **Robert, Na'ima B.** Ramadan Moon. illus. by Shirin Adl. Frances Lincoln. 2009. Tr $17.95. ISBN 978-1-84507-922-2.
K-Gr 4–Free-verse text and mixed-media collage illustrations create a satisfying depiction of Ramadan and Eid-ul-Fitr. A girl describes the excitement of the holidays, the visits to the mosque, good deeds, acts of charity, and breaking of bad habits, all of which are part of the observance.

E Hol, day. **Wildsmith, Brian.** The Easter Story. illus. by the author. Eerdmans. 2004. Knopf. 1994. Tr $20. ISBN 978-0-802-85189-5.
K-Gr 4–Gorgeous jewel-toned panoramic artwork accented with gold depicts the events of the Passion, Crucifixion, and Resurrection of Jesus Christ. The story is told from the point of view of Jesus' donkey, allowing for a childlike simplicity in the text. A visually stunning introduction to a major Christian holiday.

AUTUMN TO EARLY WINTER

○ **Brenner, Tom.** And Then Comes Halloween. illus. by Holly Meade. Candlewick. 2009. Tr $16.99. ISBN 978-0-7636-3659-3.
K-Gr 2–Poetic text and watercolor and collage illustrations create an atmospheric picture of Halloween. Sensory descriptions evoke the fall weather and children's anticipation as they carve pumpkins, decorate houses, and prepare costumes. Both spooky and sweet, just like the holiday itself.

○ **Gilmore, Rachna.** Lights for Gita. illus. by Alice Priestley. Second Story Press. 1995. pap. $7.95. ISBN 978-0-929005-61-4.
Gr 1-4–New Canadian Gita misses the Divali celebrations back home in New Delhi. An ice storm knocks out power and nixes plans for fireworks that celebrate this Hindu "festival of lights." Looking at the diyas (oil lamps), she remembers the holiday's meaning of finding light within ourselves. Gentle watercolors bring Gita's home to life.

E
Holiday **Goode, Diane.** Thanksgiving Is Here! illus. by the author. HarperCollins. 2003. Tr $17.99. ISBN 978-0-06-051588-1; pap. $6.99. ISBN 978-0-06-051590-4.
PreS-Gr 3–An extended family gathers to talk, play, make music, hug, and eat Grandma's turkey dinner. Amusing subplots are hidden within the buzz of activity in the detailed pen-and-ink and watercolor cartoons. This story is as warm and joyful as the holiday itself.

○ **Jules, Jacqueline.** Duck for Turkey Day. illus. by Kathryn Mitter. Albert Whitman. 2009. Tr $16.99. ISBN 978-0-8075-1734-5.
Gr 1-4–Tuyet's class enjoys turkey crafts and turkey songs, so her Vietnamese-American family's Thanksgiving duck worries her. Post-Thanksgiving, she is surprised to discover that many classmates ate alternatives, from lamb to enchiladas. Sweetly illustrated, this story shows that the heart of the holiday is family togetherness and gratitude.

○ **Jules, Jacqueline.** The Hardest Word: A Yom Kippur Story. illus by Katherine Janus Kahn. Kar-Ben. 2001. pap. $7.95. ISBN 978-1-580-13028-8.
PreS-Gr 4–God asks the mythical Ziz bird to search for "the hardest word" to make amends for smashing the children's garden. Defeated, the Ziz apologizes and discovers that the hardest word is "sorry," the word all say on Yom Kippur to atone for wrongdoings. Charming cartoon artwork keeps the tone playful despite the serious message.

E
Holiday **Katz, Karen.** My First Kwanzaa. illus. by the author. Henry Holt. 2003. RTE $14.95. ISBN 978-0-805-07077-4.
PreS-Gr 2–Brightly hued collage and mixed-media illustrations pop with joy in this buoyant introduction to the African-American harvest holiday. Narrated by a smiling little girl surrounded by loving extended family and friends, she explains how seven candles lit over seven days each celebrate a particular principle of Kwanzaa.

Kontis, Alethea. Alpha Oops! H Is for Halloween. illus. by Bob Kolar. Candlewick. 2010. RTE $15.99. ISBN 978-0-7636-3966-2.

K-Gr 3–Alphabet letters, randomly ordered, show off their costumes: "Z is for zombie. N is for nightmare," and so on. Poor B's buccaneer costume is stolen by P for pirate, but B gets the final word: "BOO!" Glowing nighttime pictures add zest to the funny, spooky tale.

Miller, Pat. Squirrel's New Year's Resolution. illus. by Kathi Ember. Albert Whitman. 2010. Tr $16.99. ISBN 978-0-8075-7591-8.

PreS-Gr 2–Squirrel wants to make a resolution, "a promise you make to yourself to be better or to help others." As she walks through the woods, pausing to cheer up Skunk, assist Mole and Turtle, and joke with Porcupine, Squirrel realizes that she can help someone every day. Cheery acrylic illustrations reflect the tone.

Musleah, Rahel. Apples and Pomegranates: A Family Seder for Rosh Hashanah. illus. by Judy Jarrett. Kar-Ben Publishing. 2004. pap. $7.95. ISBN 978-1-580-13123-0.

Gr 2-6–A mix of history, blessings, songs, and stories guides readers in creating their own celebrations for the Jewish New Year. Rosh Hashanah traditions from many lands are described, and symbolic foods are incorporated into the observance. Recipes are included, encouraging participation. Autumnal watercolor illustrations create a joyful atmosphere.

Old, Wendie. The Halloween Book of Facts and Fun. illus. by Paige Billin-Frye. Albert Whitman. 2007. Tr $15.95. ISBN 978-0-8075-3133-4.

Gr 2-4–An excellent resource for understanding the holiday more fully, this short chapter book is packed with information about history and customs. Cartoon-style illustrations and silly jokes keep the material kid-friendly even though some of the historical information is quite dark. Back matter includes recipes, party games, and safety tips.

Verma, Jatinder, retel. The Story of Divaali. illus. by Nilesh Mistry. Barefoot. 2002. Tr $16.99. ISBN 978-1-841-48936-0; pap. $7.99. ISBN 978-1-846-86131-4.

Gr 2-4–Verma focuses his retelling of *The Ramayana* on "that of the fifteenth-century poet Tulsidass." The complicated, action-packed tale may prove somewhat hard to follow for readers new to the epic, but the story conveys universal themes of bravery and the triumph of love over evil. Gouache paintings are highlighted with fascinating detail.

Wayland, April Halprin. New Year at the Pier: A Rosh Hashanah Story. illus. by Stéphane Jorisch. Dial. 2009. Tr $16.99. ISBN 978-0-8037-3279-7.

K-Gr 3–Izzy's family and congregation celebrate the Jewish New Year by asking forgiveness from those they have wronged during the year and with a Tashlich ceremony in which they symbolically cast away their sins by throwing bread into the water. Light-filled watercolors and a buoyant text keep the potentially heavy topic child-friendly.

Winter, Jeanette. Calavera Abecedario: a Day of the Dead Alphabet Book. illus. by the author. Harcourt. 2004. Tr $16. ISBN 978-0-152-05110-5; pap. $7.99. ISBN 978-0-152-05906-4.
K-Gr 4–Within a frame story of a family celebration is a friendly skeleton-themed alphabet offering words and characters related to the culture and holiday. A Spanish glossary and author's note provide background about the holiday. Vibrant artwork evokes Mexican folk art.

ALL YEAR ROUND

Allen, Nancy Kelly. "Happy Birthday": The Story of the World's Most Popular Song. illus. by Gary Undercuffler. Pelican. 2010. Tr $16.99. ISBN 978-1-58980-675-7.
Gr 1-3–Kentucky sisters Mildred and Patty Hill wrote songs together as children and adults. As schoolteachers, they began their days with their own composition, "Good Morning to All." A change of words brought about "Happy Birthday to You." Cheerful drawings show the energetic sisters' impact on their community, and ultimately, the world.

Huget, Jennifer LaRue. The Best Birthday Party Ever. illus. by LeUyen Pham. Random. 2011. Tr $16.99. ISBN 978-0-375-84763-9; PLB $19.99. ISBN 978-0-375-95763-5.
K-Gr 2–A girl is excited about her birthday, "5 months, 3 weeks, 2 days, and 8 hours" away. Outrageously snowballing party plans include magicians, rides, mounds of ice

cream, and live hamsters as party favors, yet her modest party turns out to be perfect. Colorful, dynamic illustrations capture the anticipatory fun.

MEDIA PICKS

Holidays for Children (Series). 26 DVDs. range: 12-23 min. with tchr's. guides. Library Video Co. 1994. $389.35 ser., $14.98 ea.

PreS-Gr 3–A lively mix of live-action, simple animation, photography, puppets, clever graphics, and still pictures combine to explain the meaning and history of 26 holidays including Cinco de Mayo, Chinese New Year, Hannukah, Kwanzaa, Christmas, Halloween, Rosh Hashanah/Yom Kippur, Earth Day, Arbor Day, Presidents' Day, and many more. Music, food, and dance, as well as traditional musical instruments from the highlighted culture, are presented.

National Observances (American History for Children Series). DVD. 25 min. with tchr's. guide. Library Video Co. 1996. $14.98.

Gr 1-4–This program, featuring animation, live-action footage, and sing-along songs, explains why we celebrate Veterans Day, Memorial Day, Labor Day, Independence Day, and Election Day.

Winter Holiday Stories. DVD. 27 min. Weston Woods. 2001. ISBN 978-1-555-92970-1. $59.95.

PreS-Gr 3–Includes three animated/iconographic holiday tales based on award-winning children's books: *In the Month of Kislev* by Nina Jaffe, Andrea Davis Pinkney's *Seven Candles for Kwanzaa*, and *The Night Before Christmas* by Clement C. Moore.

ON THE WEB

For Teachers

Diversity Calendar. www3.kumc.edu/diversity. The University of Kansas Medical Center. Kansas City, KS. (Accessed 6/19/14).

Developed by the Medical Center's Human Resources division, this searchable month-by-month listing of holidays around the world can be sorted by ethnic/religious celebrations, national holidays, and other events. Selected entries link to brief descriptive information or to other relevant websites.

PBS: Holidays. www.pbs.org/topics/culture-society/holidays-celebrations. PBS. (Accessed 6/19/14).

Dynamic links list updates with public television programming related to the current holiday season. From "Backyard Grilling" to "Lords of the Gourd," articles, videos, and recipes are displayed according to their relevant content.

timeanddate.com. timeanddate.com. Time and Date AS. (Accessed 6/19/14). Customizable world clocks and calendars, astronomical information, and background on holidays in diverse countries are the highlights of this extensive Norway-based site. Coverage varies, but holidays in major English-speaking countries get thorough treatment.

For Students

TOPICS Online Magazine for Learners of English. topics-mag.com/internatl/holidays/
  festivals.htm. Sandy and Thomas Peters. (Accessed 6/19/14).
Gr 2-5–This online magazine for English-language learners includes an extensive section on world holidays. The essays were written by students (new submissions always accepted), giving the site a more experiential than informational feel. The simple layout and grassroots approach are highly engaging.

Winter Celebrations. kids.nationalgeographic.com/kids/stories/peopleplaces/win-
  ter-celebrations. National Geographic Society. (Accessed 6/19/14).
Gr 2-5–Brief descriptions of holidays and traditions celebrated during December and January, including Chinese New Year, Eid al-Adha, Kwanzaa, Three Kings, Day and others, are featured along with practical suggestions for making "the season a little brighter for others."

Social Sciences

Cole, Joanna. The Magic School Bus and the Climate Challenge. 40 pp. Scholastic
  2010. ISBN 978-0-590-10826-3. Illustrated by Bruce Degen.
In the magic school bus (temporarily a plane), Ms. Frizzle's class gathers information for a play about climate change. Cole and Degen are straightforward about the seriousness of global warming but eschew gloom and doom, focusing on day-to-day changes individuals can make. Prolific sidebars provide background information, deepening the discussion and empowering the book's audience. Throughout, humor keeps readers engaged.
Pollution and Conservation; Environment—Greenhouse effect; Global warming; Energy; Environment—Conservation—Natural resources

J
323. **Evans, Shane W.** We March. 32 pp. Roaring Brook/Porter 2012. ISBN 978-1-59643-539-1.
A mother and father rouse their children from bed, pray at their local church, board a bus, march on the Mall, and listen to Dr. King speak at the Lincoln Memorial during the March on Washington. Small touches clearly anchor the story within the experiences of a child, while quietly dramatic full-bleed, double-page illustrations bring context to the minimalist text.
Government/Economics/and Education; Washington (DC); Race relations; African Americans; Civil rights; King, Martin Luther, Jr.; Activism

○ **George, Jean Craighead.** The Buffalo Are Back. 32 pp. Dutton 2010. ISBN 978-0-525-42215-0. llustrated by Wendell Minor.
In George's compact ecodrama, we first see the buffalo slaughtered to decimate the Indians and open the prairie to settlers. Moving to the somber Dust Bowl migrants, we then turn to the reversal: the discovery, instigated by President Theodore Roosevelt, of three hundred remaining wild buffalo. With illustrations that both document and dramatize, it's another small triumph from a seasoned team. Websites. Bib.
Pollution and Conservation; Environment—Endangered species; Animals—Buffalo; West (U.S.); Environment—Conservation—Wildlife

○ **Jenkins, Martin.** Can We Save the Tiger? 56 pp. Candlewick 2011. ISBN 978-0-7636-4909-8. Illustrated by Vicky White.
This volume provides a gracefully organized overview of how some of our endangered fellow creatures are doing. Jenkins's narrative voice is engagingly informal and lucid. White's pencil and oil paint illustrations fill the large pages; the pictures are mostly in sober black and white with occasional blushes of color. A stunningly beautiful book as well as an eloquent appeal and consciousness raiser. Websites. Ind.
Pollution and Conservation; Environment—Endangered species; Animals; Environment—Conservation—Wildlife

J
728 **Laroche, Giles.** If You Lived Here: Houses of the World. 32 pp. Houghton (Houghton Mifflin Trade and Reference Division) 2011. ISBN 978-0-547-23892-0.
Laroche's bas-relief cut-paper collages illustrate sixteen different dwellings that people call home, from log cabins and tree houses to pueblos and yurts. Each is introduced with a paragraph that begins with the phrase, "If you lived here," enticing readers to imagine how it might be. Facts and additional comments on each page stimulate curiosity and expand and broaden readers' worldview.
Customs and Holidays; Dwellings; Multicultural books

Simon, Seymour. Global Warming. 32 pp. HarperCollins/Collins (HarperCollins) 2010. ISBN 978-0-06-114250-5. LE ISBN 978-0-06-114251-2.

With his outstandingly straightforward and logical prose, Simon leads novices through such tricky concepts as greenhouse gases and the differences between observable daily weather and long-term climate change. The book ends with the reassurance that we can help reverse the rate of change. Full-page photographs range from decorative enhancements to comparative evidence of the effects of a rise in global average temperature. Websites. Glos., ind.

Pollution and Conservation; Global warming; Environment—Greenhouse effect

Smith, David J. If the World Were a Village: A Book About the World's People. 32 pp. Kids Can 2011. ISBN 978-1-55453-595-8. Illustrated by Shelagh Armstrong. New ed., 2002.

This updated second edition asks readers to imagine "the whole population of the world as a village of just 100 people," with each person representing sixty-nine million people (it was sixty-two million in the previous edition). Smith covers topics such as nationalities, languages, food, etc. Accurately detailed acrylic art illustrates the thought-provoking book.

Social Issues; Economics; Population

· ·

—FOCUS ON—
Class Trips
Field Day
By Joy Fleishhacker

A former SLJ staffer, Joy Fleishhacker is a freelance writer and youth services librarian at Pikes Peak Library District in Colorado.

· ·

Brown-bag lunches and bus buddies. Headcounts, lineups, and helpful chaperones. Chatter charged with anticipation and the eye-opening wonder of new experiences. Wherever a class may roam, excursions beyond the school walls provide an array of educational opportunities and plenty of excitement for students. Preparations before field trips and discussion and guided classroom projects afterward are important parts of the learning process and help youngsters to integrate and master new information, see themselves as hands-on explorers, and amp up the fun.

The books presented here have been chosen to support and enhance expeditions to favorite elementary-aged destinations: farms and other food-producing enterprises; museums (both natural history and art); nature reserves and outdoor-observation areas; community institutions; and zoos and aquariums. A mix of fact-filled offerings and fictional adventures, all of these titles pair handsome illustrations with well-written texts to entice young readers and listeners. They can be used in the classroom to support Common Core Standards by introducing and/or reviewing site-related subject matter and vocabulary as a starting point for post-trip research projects and to inspire creative art and writing projects and initiate personal written and oral narratives. Featuring class expeditions of all kinds, the titles can also be shared to generate discussion of behavioral dos and don'ts, model positive information-seeking methods, and dispel any fears or anxieties about going to unfamiliar places.

Best of all, these appealing volumes encapsulate the magic of a field-trip experience and expand the learning–and enjoyment–well beyond the designated outing.

FARM FORAYS

Cooper, Elisha. Farm. illus. by author. Scholastic/Orchard. 2010. Tr $17.99. ISBN 978-0-545-07075-1.

K-Gr 4–From springtime's busy preparations to the after-harvest autumn lull, an industrious family, including the children, sees to the workings of their modern-day farm. Cooper's elegant, loose-lined artwork depicts broad vistas and small-size close-ups, and his narrative twinkles with nitty-gritty imagery, sensory details, and gentle humor. An enlightening and enchanting overview.

Formento, Alison. These Bees Count. illus. by Sarah Snow. Albert Whitman. 2012. Tr $16.99. ISBN 978-0-8075-7868-1.

K-Gr 2–During a trip to Busy Bee Farm, Mr. Tate and his students don protective gear and learn how the insects produce honey and pollinate plants. This exquisitely illustrated offering merges fact and fancy as the bees zip into the air and buzz a rhythmic counting song while visiting a plethora of spring-hued blooms.

Holub, Joan. Pumpkin Countdown. illus. by Jan Smith. Albert Whitman. 2012. Tr $16.99. ISBN 978-0-8075-6660-2.

K-Gr 2–Bouncy rhymes and eye-dazzling artwork depict an enjoyable jaunt to Farmer Mixenmatch's pumpkin patch, complete with a petting zoo, corn maze, tractor ride, and oodles of objects to search for. Holub and Smith's *Apple Countdown* (Albert Whitman, 2009) presents a similar synthesis of simple math challenges, interesting facts, and irresistible enthusiasm.

McNamara, Margaret. The Apple Orchard Riddle. illus. by G. Brian Karas. Random/Schwartz & Wade. 2013. Tr $15.99. ISBN 978-0-375-84744-8; lib. ed. $18.99. ISBN 978-0-375-95744-4; ebook $10.99. ISBN 978-0-375-98783-0.

K-Gr 2–Mr. Tiffin's students mull over a brainteaser while touring Hill's Orchard: "Show me a little red house with no windows and no door, but with a star inside." Gathering bushels of apple facts throughout the day, the children make guesses galore, but only the quietly observant class daydreamer gets to the riddle's core. Personality-packed artwork spices up this winning tale.

Malnor, Carol L. & Trina L. Hunner. Molly's Organic Farm. illus. by Trina L. Hunner. Dawn. 2012. Tr $16.95. ISBN 978-1-58469-166-2; pap. $8.95. ISBN 978-158469-167-9.

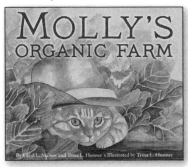

K-Gr 4–As an orange-striped stray explores a community farm, inviting text introduces the gentle-on-nature methods organic farmers employ to nurture a healthy growing environment and manage pests and weeds. Children will be charmed by the cat's-eye viewpoint, verdant watercolors, and staccato rhymes scattered throughout ("Catching whiffs./Molly sniffs"). Activity ideas and photos of the real-life Molly are appended.

Peterson, Cris. Fantastic Farm Machines. photos by David R. Lundquist. Boyds Mills. 2006. Tr $17.95. ISBN 978-1-59078-271-2.

K-Gr 4–A first-person narrative introduces the Herculean heavy machinery used on Peterson's family's farm, from chisel plow to corn planter, irrigation pivot to crop sprayer. Mixing visual detail with lighthearted fun, Lundquist's first-rate photos include portraits of charismatic youngsters (one boy lounges inside an enormous tractor tire), crystal-clear close-ups, and shots of these amazing contraptions in action.

○ **Plourde, Lynn.** Field Trip Day. illus. by Thor Wickstrom. Dutton. 2010. Tr $16.99. ISBN 978-0-525-47994-9.

K-Gr 3–Although the intrepid Juan Dore-Nomad repeatedly wanders away from his classmates, keeping a frenzied Mrs. Shepherd and her parent chaperones constantly counting heads, the boy's questions and observations lead to a lot of discoveries about Fandangle's Organic Farm. Spirited watercolor-and-ink cartoons, zippy text, and over-the-top antics will keep readers smiling.

Wallace, Nancy Elizabeth. Apples, Apples, Apples. illus. by author. Winslow. 2000. Tr $15.95 ISBN 978-1-890817-19-0; pap. $5.95. ISBN 978-0-7614-5181-5.

PreS-Gr 2–Minna and her family visit Long Hill Orchard where they learn about how apples are grown, different varieties, proper picking techniques, and yummy foods. Cleanly designed collages depict engaging rabbit characters, and clear charts and diagrams support the lively text. A recipe, apple-printing craft, and song are appended.

Watterson, Carol. An Edible Alphabet: 26 Reasons to Love the Farm. illus. by Michela Sorrentino. Tricycle. 2011. Tr $16.99. ISBN 978-1-58246-421-3.

Gr 1-4–Bursting with wordplay and whimsy, this exuberantly illustrated A-to-Z provides a bounty of intriguing facts and helps readers make the connection between food and farm. Letters are accompanied by alliterative snippets ("Blueberries, Beets, and Beans") while smaller-size text introduces the featured plants, animals, or agricultural process. A captivating read-aloud or invigorating idea-starter for creative projects.

MUSEUM MEANDERINGS

○ **Hartland, Jessie.** How the Sphinx Got to the Museum. illus. by author. Blue Apple. 2010. Tr $17.99. ISBN 978-1-60905-032-0.

Gr 1-4–Step by mesmerizing step, this picture book reveals how a statue commissioned by Pharaoh Hatshepsut circa 1470 B.C. made its way centuries later to New York's Metropolitan Museum of Art. The cadenced text and vivacious artwork effortlessly–and entertainingly–delve into ancient Egyptian history, the museum's acquisition process, and careers ranging from archaeologist to conservator. Similarly presented, *How the Dinosaur Got to the Museum* (Blue Apple, 2011) traces a *Diplodocus*'s journey to the Smithsonian.

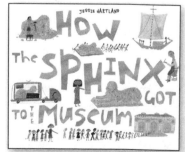

Hopkins, Lee Bennett, sel. Behind the Museum Door: Poems to Celebrate the Wonders of Museums. illus. by Stacey Dressen-McQueen. Abrams. 2007. Tr $16.95. ISBN 978-0-8109-1204-5.

Gr 3-5–From Felice Holman's musings about how portraits reveal details of long-ago lives to Alice Shertle's ode to a trilobite, 14 selections showcase commonly exhibited marvels. Jewel-toned paintings interpret each poem with realistic details and fanciful touches. This handsome anthology will have youngsters viewing museums and their treasures with fresh eyes.

Lehman, Barbara. Museum Trip. illus. by author. Houghton Harcourt. 2006. Tr $15. ISBN 978-0-618-58125-2; ebook $15. ISBN 978-0-547-77086-4.

K-Gr 4–Separated from his school group, a boy lingers over an exhibit of antique mazes and suddenly finds himself shrunk down and inside the display case. Zoomed-in illustrations show him conquering six twisting-turning labyrinths and receiving a gold medal, which he still wears–wondrously, mysteriously–when he rejoins his classmates. This winsome wordless adventure blurs the lines between reality and imagination.

Mark, Jan. The Museum Book: A Guide to Strange and Wonderful Collections. illus. by Richard Holland. Candlewick. 2007. RTE $18.99. ISBN 978-0-7636-3370-7.

Gr 3-6–Chronicling the ages-old human passion for collecting "interesting" things, Mark's look at the history of museums touches upon everything from famous hoarders of yore to the origins of scientific classification and modern-day institutions. The conversational text and mixed-media collage artwork make this miscellany of amazing anecdotes and intriguing insights perfect for sharing aloud.

Raczka, Bob. More Than Meets the Eye: Seeing Art with All Five Senses. Millbrook. 2003. lib. ed. $25.26. ISBN 978-0-7613-2797-4; pap. $9.95. ISBN 978-0-7613-1994-8.

Gr 1-4–Rhyming text paired with striking reproductions encourages readers to utilize the senses when contemplating paintings. Kids drink milk with Jan Vermeer's *Kitchen Maid*, listen to the clashing foils of Milton Avery's *Fencers*, catch a "stinky" whiff from Jamie Wyeth's *Portrait of a Pig*, and pat the *Tortilla-Maker*'s floury treat (Diego Rivera). This simple yet imagination-expanding method of experiencing art will captivate youngsters.

E R

Rohmann, Eric. Time Flies. illus. by author. Crown. 1994. Tr $17. ISBN 978-0-517-59598-5; pap. $6.99. ISBN 978-0-517-88555-0.

PreS-Gr 4–In this wordless picture book, a bird flies into a museum's dinosaur hall during a storm-charged night. Suddenly, time slips away–the walls disappear, the gigantic skeletons become fully fleshed-out behemoths roaming a prehistoric landscape, and the bird is placed in peril. This gorgeously illustrated flight of fancy can inspire creative endeavors or paleontological research.

NATURE WALKS

J 508 A

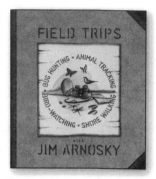

Arnosky, Jim. Field Trips: Bug Hunting, Animal Tracking, Bird-Watching, and Shore Walking with Jim Arnosky. illus. by author. HarperCollins. 2002. Tr $17.99. ISBN 978-0-688-15172-0.

Gr 3-5–This basic guide to outdoor rambling covers wildlife spotting and observation, animal behaviors, equipment and safety measures, and how-to tips for recording discoveries in a field notebook. Realistic drawings and silhouette charts of plants, animals, and tracks aid readers with species identification. Arnosky's mélange of practical lore and heartfelt fervor is informative and inspiring.

O

Harper, Jamie. Miss Mingo Weathers the Storm. illus. by author. Candlewick. 2012. RTE $15.99. ISBN 978-0-7636-4931-9.

Gr 1-3–The unflappable flamingo and her multispecies class hike to a meteorological observatory atop High Hill, where they encounter everything from hot temperatures to high winds to hailstones and learn about the weather and how animals react to changing conditions. This whirlwind adventure sparkles with humor and lush artwork.

ER P

Parish, Herman. Amelia Bedelia Hits the Trail. illus. by Lynne Avril. HarperCollins/Greenwillow. 2013. Tr $16.99. ISBN 978-0-06-209527-5; pap. $3.99. ISBN 978-0-06-209526-8; ebook $4.99. ISBN 978-0-06-209528-2.

PreS-Gr 2–Starring an updated but still literal-minded childhood version of the beloved character, this easy reader describes a nature excursion during which Amelia Bedelia follows her teacher's instructions to the letter, embarking on a fun- and pun-filled adventure. The protagonist's upbeat perseverance is just as sunny as the buoyant cartoon artwork.

Wallace, Nancy Elizabeth. Pond Walk. illus. by author. Marshall Cavendish. 2011. Tr $17.99. ISBN 978-0-7614-5816-6.

PreS-Gr 3–An endearing bear and his mother visit Pete's Pond to observe, identify, and investigate animals, insects, and plants. The crisp collage illustrations incorporate photos of flora and fauna, and the young naturalist's childlike colored-pencil drawings of specimens are scattered throughout. Warmed with gentle humor, Wallace's charmer presents an informative overview and a helpful model for exploration.

NEIGHBORHOOD RAMBLES

Bertram, Debbie & Susan Bloom. The Best Book to Read. illus. by Michael Garland. Random. 2008. Tr $14.99. ISBN 978-0-375-84702-8; lib. ed. $17.99. ISBN 978-0-375-94702-5; pap. $6.99. ISBN 978-0-375-87300-3.

K-Gr 3–An effervescent librarian welcomes a class, highlights various genres of books along with kid-grabbing titles (about dragon-battling, cake-baking, magic-making, and more), and invites the youngsters to browse. Jaunty rhymes and color-drenched digital illustrations depict a just-right library visit that culminates with a busload of kids who can't wait to get reading.

Bourgeois, Paulette. Postal Workers. illus. by Kim LaFave. Kids Can. 2005. pap. $5.95. ISBN 978-1-55337-747-4.

K-Gr 2–In this easy reader, accessible text and soft-edged cartoon artwork outline the route Gordon's birthday card takes from a Canadian post office to Grandma's mailbox in Oregon, a journey that involves automated and human sorters, trucks and planes, and a smiling letter carrier. A companion volume provides an equally charming look at firefighters (Kids Can, 2005).

Krull, Kathleen. Supermarket. illus. by Melanie Hope Greenberg. Holiday House. 2001. Tr $17.95. ISBN 978-0-8234-1546-5.

PreS-Gr 3–Lively text and dynamic gouache paintings provide an aisle-by-aisle overview of this distinctly American invention, discussing the history of supermarkets, how they are organized, customer shopping habits, and assorted food facts.

Well-stocked with amusing touches, this accessible picture book also conveys the store's role as family destination and community stopping place.

Murray, Laura. The Gingerbread Man Loose on the Fire Truck. illus. by Mike Lowery. Putnam. 2013. Tr $16.99. ISBN 978-0-399-25779-7.

PreS-Gr 1–In his second adventure, the irrepressible cookie joins the students who created him on a visit to the fire station, where his efforts to avoid a Dalmatian's snapping jaws result in a wild chase and a heart- and hose-pumping finale. Energetic cartoons, rhyming text, and hilarious antics make this a kid-pleasing read-aloud.

Slate, Joseph. Miss Bindergarten Takes a Field Trip. illus. by Ashley Wolff. Dutton. 2001. Tr $16.99. ISBN 978-0-525-46710-6; pap. $6.99. ISBN 978-0-14-240139-2.

PreS-Gr 2–The affable canine teacher takes her kindergarteners on a neighborhood tour with stops at a bakery, fire station, post office, library, and park (for a picnic). Spanning the alphabet from Adam the alligator to Zack the zebra, rhyming verses and bright-hued illustrations reveal the adventures of the likable characters, and an appended search-for-the-shape feature adds to the fun.

ZOO AND AQUARIUM EXPEDITIONS

Aliki. My Visit to the Zoo. illus. by author. HarperCollins. 1997. Tr $17.99. ISBN 978-0-06-024939-7; pap. $6.99. ISBN 978-0-06-446217-4.

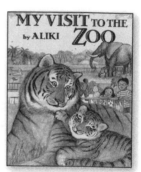

K-Gr 3–As they ramble through a zoo's wooded grounds and well-maintained habitats, two youngsters learn about the animal inhabitants and their natural environments, conservation and ecological issues, and the park's role as wildlife sanctuary. Told in first-person text brimming with childlike charm, this stunningly illustrated volume is a perfect field trip primer. See also *My Visit to the Aquarium* (HarperCollins, 1993).

Harvey, Jeanne Walker. Astro: The Steller Sea Lion. illus. by Shennen Bersani. Sylvan Dell. 2010. Tr $16.99. ISBN 978-1-60718-076-0; pap. $8.95. ISBN 978-1-60718-087-6.

K-Gr 4–Orphaned, rescued, and raised by Marine Mammal Center staffers in California, a sea lion pup is released into the ocean with high hopes, but after he returns time and time again to shore—and human companionship—his caregivers must come up with an alternate plan. This touching based-in-fact story is illustrated with expansive photorealistic paintings.

Ⓐ **Hatkoff, Juliana, Isabella Hatkoff, & Craig Hatkoff.** Leo the Snow Leopard: The True Story of an Amazing Rescue. Scholastic. 2010. Tr $17.99. ISBN 978-0-545-22927-2.
K-Gr 5–Found by a goatherd in Pakistan's rugged mountains, an orphaned cub began an arduous journey to his future home at New York's Bronx Zoo. This upbeat true tale conveys how caring individuals from different nations collaborated to save an endangered animal and demonstrates a zoo's role in wildlife rehabilitation and conservation.

Ⓞ **Komiya, Teruyuki,** ed. Life-Size Zoo: From Tiny Rodents to Gigantic Elephants, An Actual-Size Animal Encyclopedia. photos by Toyofumi Fukuda. 2008. Tr $17.95. ISBN 978-1-934734-20-9.
_____. More Life-Size Zoo: An All-New Actual-Size Animal Encyclopedia. photos by Toshimitsu Matsuhashi. 2010. Tr $18.95. ISBN 978-1-934734-19-3.
ea vol: Seven Footer.
K-Gr 3–Displaying superb photos of favorite zoo animals on eye-catching spreads (and several dramatic foldouts), these books mix close-up head shots of larger species (elephant, aardvark, lion, etc.) with full-body images of smaller creatures (koala, sloth, bat). Entries include chatty intros, "can you find" prompts for closer observation, and fun facts. All-around browsers' delights, these oversize volumes are useful for prepping for or revisiting a zoo.

J
808.81 **Lewis, J. Patrick,** ed. National Geographic Book of Animal Poetry: 200 Poems with Photographs That Squeak, Soar, and Roar! National Geographic. 2012. Tr $24.95. ISBN 978-1-4263-1009-6; lib. ed. $28.95. ISBN 978-1-4263-1054-6.
Gr 1-5–Well-chosen poems are paired with breathtaking photos of the featured creatures, many depicted in their natural habitats. Entries vary from playful to thought-provoking, and the mixture of word and visual image is potent. Providing creative perspectives on critters from polliwogs to panthers, egrets to elephants, these selections will inspire youngsters to try penning an animal ode.

Ⓞ **Poydar, Nancy.** Fish School. illus. by author. Holiday House. 2009. Tr $16.95. ISBN 978-0-8234-2140-4.
K-Gr 3–Determined to teach his new goldfish everything he learns, Charlie zips his pet into a plastic bag and sneaks him along on an aquarium field trip. However, his secret is revealed when his backpack containing Wishy goes missing, and his caring classmates jump in to save the day. This cheerfully illustrated tale is an outing with colorful fish species, facts, and metaphors.

E
S

Scotton, Rob. Splat and the Cool School Trip. illus. by author. HarperCollins. 2013. Tr $17.99. ISBN 978-0-06-213386-1; ebook $12.99. ISBN 978-0-06-213388-5.

K-Gr 2–The endearing cat returns in another satisfyingly silly romp. It's zoo day, and Splat can't wait to see the penguins. However, when his mouse friend Seymour arrives on the scene unexpectedly, the ensuing hullabaloo results in a penguin-house closure and a disappointed kitty. Never fear, clever Seymour has an idea that brings about a brighter-than-blue-skies ending.

DIGITAL PICKS

4-H Virtual Farm. www.sites.ext.vt.edu/virtualfarm. Virginia Cooperative Extension/Virginia Tech. (Accessed 6/19/14).
Gr 2-6–From wheat producers to aquaculture, dairy cows to cattle, poultry farm to horse farm, this interactive site provides overviews of six different operations. Fun-to-explore video clips and photo/interviews with agricultural professionals, virtual tours, animations, and clear graphics convey the workings of each establishment, scientific concepts, related vocabulary, and more.

Meet Me at the Corner: Virtual Field Trips for Kids. www.meetmeatthecorner.org. Donna W. Guthrie. (Accessed 6/19/14).
K-Gr 5–Founded in 2006 by Guthrie, an educator and children's book author, this site features elucidating videos about a wide array of destinations and interesting topics. Searchable by subject categories, the kid-conducted podcasts are supplemented with background material, learning activities, and topic-related websites.

San Diego Zoo: Kids. kids.sandiegozoo.org. San Diego Zoo. (Accessed 6/19/14).
K-Gr 5–Colorful, easy-to-navigate, and packed with information, this site invites youngsters to check out live animal cams; encounter numerous species by browsing photos, videos, and clearly presented facts; investigate zoo jobs; play games; and try their hand at drawing activities and craft projects.

Virtual NMNH Museum Tour: Dinosaurs. www.paleobiology.si.edu/dinosaurs. Smithsonian National Museum of Natural History. (Accessed 6/19/14).
Gr 3-6–Visitors click on objects in a virtual hall to access information about various

dinosaur species and the study of paleontology. Included are crisp fossil photos and 3-D images, a Cretaceous Period diorama, a microscope interactive for viewing specimens, and a fascinating behind-the-scenes look at the museum's extensive fossil collection.

Wackykids. www.wackykids.org/welcome.htm. Denver Art Museum. (Accessed 6/19/14).
K-Gr 3–"The wac in wacky stands for world art and cultures," explain this site's authors. It showcases several artworks–a Chinese Dragon Robe, an ancient Egyptian mummy case, a Mayan figurine, and more–along with info about the people who produced each object. Crafts, booklists, and web links are also included.

MEDIA PICKS
By Phyllis Levy Mandell

Kid Guides: Aquariums. DVD. 88 min. Thetravelingtrio.tv. 2007, 2008 release. ISBN 978-1-56839-297-4. $19.95.
Gr 1-6–Want to see through a jellyfish? Watch sharks being fed? Matt and Brittney take viewers on tours of the Downtown Aquarium in Houston, the Shedd Aquarium in Chicago, and The Monterey Bay Regional Aquarium in California. The photographs of each facility and the marine life are breathtaking.

Kid Guides: Museums. DVD. 88 min. Janson Media. 2008. ISBN 978-1-56839-298-2. $19.95.
Gr 1-6–Travel with Matt and Brittney on visits to the predominantly hands-on Franklin Institute Museum in Philadelphia where they explore a human heart, discover what gives fireworks their colors, ride a sky bike above the exhibits, and meet Ben Franklin for a fascinating lesson in the Hall of Electricity. At the International Spy Museum in Washington, DC, the hosts learn how to write and decipher codes, plant information, and more.

Kid Guides: Zoos. DVD. 1:50 hrs. Thetravelingtrio.tv. 2007. ISBN 978-1-56839-296-6. $19.95.
Gr 1-6–Tour three of the country's most exciting zoos—St. Louis Zoo, the National Zoo in Washington, DC, and the Ft. Worth Zoo in Texas. Go behind the scenes to share amazing experiences with the animals. At the end of each segment, one creature is examined in the "Explorer's Corner" and another is featured in "Star of the Week." Learn how pandas and elephants are cared for, see how keepers handle venomous snakes, participate in a sea lion show, and more.

My Fantastic Field Trip to the Planets: A Musical Adventure (rev. ed.). DVD. 90 min. CDUniverse. 2009. ISBN 0-9770520-1-X. $16.98.

K-Gr 3–A young boy takes an imaginary rocket trip into space and meets the sun and the planets. The bonus bits are the real strength of this production. They include some wonderful featurettes from NASA about the history of space travel, life in orbit, a tour of the International Space Station, and more. Updated to reflect the change in Pluto's standing.

· ·

—FOCUS ON—

Amazing Journeys

Going Places

By John Peters

John Peters is a Children's Literature Consultant in New York City.

· ·

"**T**raveling—it leaves you speechless, then turns you into a storyteller." So writes the narrator in *Traveling Man: The Journey of Ibn Battuta, 1325-1354,* James Rumford's picture-book introduction to the greatest travel writer of the 14th (or, for that matter, probably any) century.

Whether undertaken from simple restlessness or curiosity about the world, in hopes of finding a better life, to flee war or natural disaster, or simply to go where no one has gone before, travel creates experiences and memories that not only change the traveler but, in the right hands, also become some of our finest and most enthralling stories.

Here is a mix of odysseys real and imaginary, published for the most part within the past decade, that will captivate readers with both the lure of new and exotic locales and the hazards and rewards of the journeys themselves.

OVER LANDS AND SEAS

Brown, Don. Uncommon Traveler: Mary Kingsley in Africa. illus. by author. Houghton Harcourt. 2000. Tr $16.99. ISBN 978-0-618-00273-3; pap. $6.95. ISBN 978-0-618-36916-4; ebook $6.95. ISBN 978-0-547-77276-9.

Gr 2-4–Forced by family obligations to stay at home for most of her first 30 years, Victorian Mary Kingsley made a most unlikely candidate for the role of intrepid explorer. Once free to do so, though, she set out for the remote areas of Africa that she had only read about. Fluid watercolor illustrations underscore the drama of her adventures.

Burleigh, Robert. Night Flight: Amelia Earhart Crosses the Atlantic. illus. by Wendell Minor. S & S. 2011. Tr $16.99. ISBN 978-1-416-96733-0.
Gr 2-4–In an extreme test of determination, nerve, and skill, a flier sets out on a 2000-mile solo flight across the ocean. With equal drama, the text and the pictures combine to capture the flight's long hours of danger and uncertainty, as well as the renowned aviator's steady courage.

Evans, Shane W. Underground: Finding the Light to Freedom. illus. by author. Roaring Brook/A Neal Porter Bk. 2011. Tr $16.99. ISBN 978-1-596-43538-4.
Gr 3-5–In a hushed, terse text and illustrations done in dark blues with stark flashes of white later changing to golds to signal terror's end and the Sun's rising, this powerful picture book follows a family making an urgent, danger-filled journey from slavery to freedom.

Judge, Chris. The Lonely Beast. illus. by author. Andersen, dist. by Lerner. 2011. Tr $16.95. ISBN 978-0-761-38097-9.
Gr 1-3–Prompted by a need for companionship, a monster, depicted as a huge, hairy, enigmatic black silhouette in Judge's cartoon illustrations, leaves its familiar forest and sets out on a quest that takes it over many lands, under oceans, and into various adventures with a happy surprise waiting at the end.

Ross, Stewart. Into the Unknown: How Great Explorers Found Their Way by Land, Sea, and Air. illus. by Stephen Biesty. Candlewick. 2011. Tr $19.99. ISBN 978-0-763-64948-7.
Gr 3-6–Biesty's fantastically detailed illustrations, several on foldouts, highlight this gathering of great voyages and epic quests. From the travels of Chinese explorer Zheng He to the expeditions of David Livingstone, from the deep sea dives of Jacques Piccard to the flights of his father, balloonist Auguste Piccard, there is adventure aplenty to inspire real or imaginary travels.

Shulevitz, Uri. The Travels of Benjamin of Tudela: Through Three Continents in the Twelfth Century. illus. by author. Farrar. 2005. Tr $17. ISBN 978-0-374-37754-0.

Gr 2-5–Enhanced with period-style scenes of compressed cities and of small ships being tossed on rough waters, this story of a 12th-century traveler who crossed three continents to visit every land mentioned in the Old Testament captures both the flavor of exotic lands and the terrors of going anywhere farther than one's doorstep in those troubled times.

Stead, Philip Christian. Jonathan and the Big Blue Boat. illus. by the author. Roaring Brook/A Neal Porter Bk. 2011. Tr $16.99. ISBN 978-1-596-43562-9.

Gr 1-3–When Jonathan's clueless parents trade in his beloved bear for a toaster, off he steams in a huge ship to reclaim his stuffed toy. He finds other, even more unlikely, companions along the way. A dreamy, surreal tale with appropriately quirky illustrations.

AROUND THE WORLD AND BENEATH ITS SURFACE

Burks, James. Beep and Bah. illus. by author. Carolrhoda. 2012. RTE $16.95. ISBN 978-0-761-36567-9; ebook $12.95. ISBN 978-0-7613-8721-3.

K-Gr 2–In a quest tale that sets new standards for unlikely partners, the search for a sock's misplaced companion sends a goat and a rolling robot roving far and wide. Comical cartoon illustrations depict encounters with a bull, a snake, a rock, and other equally unlikely sock owners.

Chad, Jon. Leo Geo: And His Miraculous Journey Through the Center of the Earth. illus. by author. Roaring Brook. 2012. Tr $15.99. ISBN 978-1-596-43661-9.

Gr 2-4–A series of long, skinny vertical images depicts the monstrous residents, teeming cities, and more conventional geological wonders of our planet's interior waiting for intrepid explorer Leo Geo of the Fizzmont Institute of Rad Science. A fascinating journey to the center of the Earth—and beyond.

Kelly, Irene. A Small Dog's Big Life: Around the World with Owney. illus. by author. Holiday House. 2005. RTE $16.95. ISBN 978-0-823-41863-3.

K-Gr 2–Retold in fictionalized letters, this is the true and amazing "tail" of a stray dog who was adopted by the U.S. Postal Service and went on to travel thousands of miles with the mail, not only all over North America, but around the world as well. Lively watercolor scenes featuring a bright-eyed, nondescript pooch capture his winning personality.

ABOVE (AND BEYOND) THE PLANET

McNulty, Faith. If You Decide to Go to the Moon. illus. by Steven Kellogg. Scholastic. 2005. RTE $18.99. ISBN 978-0-590-48359-9.

K-Gr 3–In a terrific blend of wish fulfillment and scientific fact, McNulty lays out what to pack for a trip to the Moon, what the journey will be like, and what a visitor might see and do on our satellite's surface. Kellogg's illustrations crank up the exuberance and provide compelling reasons for a stronger appreciation of Earth's wonders.

Taylor, Jane. Twinkle, Twinkle, Little Star. illus. by Jerry Pinkney. Little, Brown. 2011. Tr $16.99. ISBN 978-0-316-05696-0.

PreS-Gr 1–Pinkney turns the familiar bedtime rhyme into a nighttime sojourn that takes a small chipmunk from its cozy nest all the way to the Moon and back. Lush close-ups of leafy branches and other outdoor features in the artist's accomplished watercolors create natural settings as intimate as they are accurately detailed.

MEDIA PICKS

By Phyllis Levy Mandell

Henry's Freedom Box: A True Story from the Underground Railroad. DVD. 10 min. Weston Woods. 2009. ISBN 978-0-545-13438-5. $59.95; CD, ISBN 978-0-545-13445-3: $12.95; CD with hardcover book, ISBN 978-0-545-13455-2: $29.95.

Gr 2-5–One of the most interesting stories from the Underground Railroad is that of Henry "Box" Brown, raised a slave, who mailed himself to Philadelphia and freedom in a small wooden crate. Ellen Levine tells his tale (Scholastic, 2007) with well-crafted, evocative text, beautifully paired with Kadir Nelson's heart-touching illustrations that are scanned iconographically. Nicely narrated by Jerry Dixon, with original music and sound effects that help bring the story to life, the Caldecott Honor book is well-served by this presentation.

The Journey of Oliver K. Woodman. DVD. 11 min. Nutmeg Media. 2005. ISBN 0-9772-3383-9. $49.95.

K-Gr 3–Tameka lives in California but longs to see her favorite uncle, whose home is on the East coast. Uncle Ray builds a life-size wooden person, names him Oliver K. Woodman, and leaves him on the side of the road with a note asking passersby to help Oliver in his journey to reach Tameka's home. Darcy Pattison's picture book (Harcourt, 2003) presents the story via letters, and Joe Cepeda's vibrant illustrations and a musical background enrich the telling. Viewers will cheer Oliver on his journey.

Where Do You Think You're Going, Christopher Columbus? DVD. 31 min. Weston Woods. 1991. ISBN 978-0-545-02767-0. $59.95; CD, ISBN 978-0-439-72284-1: $14.95; CD with hardcover book, ISBN 978-0-439-73527-8: $29.95.
Gr 2-6–Jean Fritz's witty, unconventional look at the great explorer who accidentally discovered the New World while on a voyage to reach the Indies reveals the navigator's obstinate as well as his visionary side. Margot Tomes's illustrations are scanned iconographically and enhance this entertaining biography.

Eds. Note: The full version of "Going Places"
can be found online at http://ow.ly/yijie.

—FOCUS ON—
Playground Lessons
Social Climbers
By Alyson Low

Alyson Low is a Youth Librarian at the Fayetteville (AR) Public Library.

At its simplest, the playground is where kids can kick at the clouds from the swings, but at its most complicated, it's a microcosm of the real world, with similar stresses and question marks. Children learn to conduct transactions and navigate relationships with others as they process insights into their own personalities. It can be fun, but it can be scary, sad, and frustrating, too. Surrounded by laughing and chattering playmates, kids may also feel lonely as these new aspects of life loom large. What are caregivers to do? Sharing similar childhood experiences helps, but when young eyes roll at the sound of "Well, when I was your age...," the voices of peers, as represented in the titles listed here, can make an even greater impact.

MAKING FRIENDS

Becker, Bonny. A Bedtime for Bear. illus. by Kady MacDonald Denton. Candlewick. 2010. Tr $16.99. ISBN 9780763641016.

PreS-K–Bear is ready for sleep, but Mouse won't settle down. After Bear's annoyance reaches a noisy crescendo, the little guest finishes his bedtime routine, and all is quiet—for a bit. Charming artwork makes this unlikely pair all the more endearing, and the humorous tale illustrates that true friendship takes patience and gives love in return.

Joosse, Barbara. Friends (Mostly). illus. by Tomaso Milian. HarperCollins/Greenwillow. 2010. Tr $16.99. ISBN 9780060882211.

PreS-Gr 2–With fun details and silly words like "gruffly" and "zurly," Joosse chronicles the ups and downs of friendship, demonstrating that being pals is not always smooth sailing. Joyful artwork fills the pages with energy and color, adding to a cheerful and honest look at the very next relationships after family that kids will learn to navigate.

Kelly, Mij. Friendly Day. illus. by Charles Fuge. Barron's. 2013. pap. $8.99. ISBN 9781438003450.

PreS-Gr 2–Mouse tells Cat that today is Friendly Day, so the feline cannot eat him. Cat spreads the news, and animals everywhere commit hilariously random acts of kindness. Bear reveals it was a ploy by Mouse, but suggests Friendly Day can still happen. Kids will laugh at the delightful rhymes and artwork and may be inspired to start their own Friendly Day.

Pace, Anne Marie. Vampirina Ballerina Hosts a Sleepover. illus. by LeUyen Pham. Hyperion/Disney. 2013. RTE $16.99. ISBN 9781423175704.

K-Gr 2–Tucked in amid the fun of a sleepover is a nice message about friendship and reassuring a buddy who is feeling uncertain about things, which, in this case, involves eating tentacle soup and playing with a mummy. The delightfully creepy context and comically detailed illustrations drive home the idea of enjoying all kinds of friends.

Willems, Mo. Leonardo, the Terrible Monster. illus. by author. Hyperion/Disney. 2005. RTE $16.99. ISBN 9780786852949.

PreS-Gr 2–To prove that he really is a terrible—as in scary, not inept—monster, Leonardo finds a victim in pitiful little Sam. Leonardo takes credit for Sam's tears, but when the boy unloads his issues, the monster realizes he has a higher purpose. With his trademark minimalist humor in words and art, Willems delivers a satisfying message about friendship. Audio and video versions available from Weston Woods.

CELEBRATING UNIQUENESS

Burstein, John. Can We Get Along?: Dealing with Differences. (Slim Goodbody's Life Skills 101 Series). Crabtree. 2009. lib. ed. $26.60. ISBN 9780778747888; pap. $8.95. ISBN 9780778748045.

Gr 2-5–Before recommending strategies to resolve conflict, the author highlights interesting examples of the very differences (religious, cultural, physical, etc.) that may cause it. Nearly every spread contains a reflective feature challenging kids to more closely examine their viewpoints. A positive, useful tool illustrated with color photos and drawings.

Shannon, George. Turkey Tot. illus. by Jennifer K. Mann. Holiday House. 2013. RTE $16.95. ISBN 9780823423798.

PreS-K–Turkey Tot is a resourceful, hopeful fellow who refuses to let farmyard naysayers get him down. When he conceives an out-of-the-box idea for gathering plump berries, Hen's observation that Turkey Tot "has been different since the day he was hatched" morphs from criticism to compliment. Watercolor, pencil, and digital collage illustrations pop against ample white space.

Spinelli, Eileen. When No One Is Watching. illus. by David A. Johnson. Eerdmans. 2013. Tr $16. ISBN 9780802853035.

PreS-Gr 2–An introverted little girl bubbles over with spirit and imagination, but she keeps her joyful bursts of energy to herself and her best friend for now. Spinelli's endearing protagonist encourages shy children to celebrate who and where they are right now in life. Johnson's illustrations, rendered in earthy shades, fill the pages with likable faces and activity.

Yerkes, Jennifer. A Funny Little Bird. illus. by author. Sourcebooks/Jabberwocky. 2013. Tr $15.99. ISBN 97814022 80139.

PreS-Gr 1–An invisible bird, tired of being ignored, takes measures that get him noticed but by the wrong kind of critter: a fox. When the bird is himself, however, he can hide his small friends from predators, and he realizes he should be proud of this quality. The minimal, jewel-toned artwork against abundant white space packs a wonderful punch.

DEALING WITH BULLIES

Ludwig, Trudy. Confessions of a Former Bully. illus. by Beth Adams. Tricycle. 2010. Tr $15.99. ISBN 9781582463094; pap. $7.99. ISBN 9780307931139. Gr 3-5–In trouble for bullying, Katie must make amends for the pain she has caused. She decides to turn her journal into a book to educate others about bullying. Written in a tween's voice and illustrated with cartoon drawings, Katie's musings about both sides of the problem will engage and educate the target audience.

Mullarkey, Lisa. TJ Zaps the Smackdown: Stopping a Physical Bully. illus. by Gary La-Coste. (TJ Trapper, Bully Zapper Series: Bk. 6). ABDO/Magic Wagon. 2013. lib. ed. $27.07. ISBN 9781616419103.
Gr 2-4–Kids will find themselves—and good information—in this honest, accurate take on the multiple impacts of bullying. TJ helps Ethan contend with Niko, a cruel boy on their basketball team. The story addresses verbal and physical bullying, as well as the solutions to stop it, but the message is never preachy or heavy-handed.

O'Neill, Alexis. The Recess Queen. illus. by Laura Huliska-Beith. Scholastic. 2002. Tr $16.99. ISBN 9780439206372.
K-Gr 2–Playground bully Mean Jean meets her match in Katie Sue, the spunky new kid. First unaware of and then undeterred by the Recess Queen's tyrannical rule, Katie Sue uses joy, confidence, and grace to change recess for the better. Readers will soak up O'Neill's fun writing, Huliska-Beith's rollicking, bold artwork, and the great message about courage and second chances.

Wishinsky, Frieda. A Noodle Up Your Nose. illus. by Louise-Andrée Laliberté. (Orca Echoes Series). Orca. 2004. pap. $6.95. ISBN 9781551432946.
Gr 1-3–Kate must invite her entire class to her birthday party, including Violet, who tries to ruin the festivities after a misunderstanding. A truce appears possible, but Violet resorts to her bullying ways, and Kate is certain her party is

doomed. Simple but expressive pencil sketches dot the text, and kids will identify with the characters.

LEARNING TO SHARE

Berger, Samantha. Martha Doesn't Share! illus. by Bruce Whatley. Little, Brown. 2010. Tr $16.99. ISBN 9780316073677; ebk. $9.99. ISBN 9780316186735.
PreS-K–Martha, an expressive little otter, refuses to share anything with her younger brother, but in time, she realizes toys and treats don't mean much if there's no one with whom to enjoy them. Berger reveals the rewards of savoring the good stuff with family and friends in this sweet, simple story complemented by Whatley's soft watercolor palette.

Graves, Sue. Not Fair, Won't Share. illus. by Desideria Guicciardini. (Our Emotions and Behavior Series). Free Spirit. 2011. Tr $12.99. ISBN 9781575423753.
PreS-K–Like a rock tossed in a pond, Nora's refusal to share has a ripple effect; waves of anger wash over classmates and the teacher, bringing a fun activity to a halt. Everyone takes a time-out and eventually comes back together to apologize and move forward. Colorful cartoon drawings portray the full representation of hurting and healing.

Grimes, Nikki. Almost Zero. illus. by R. Gregory Christie. (A Dyamonde Daniel Book Series). Putnam. 2010. Tr $10.99. ISBN 9780399251771; ebk. $9.99. ISBN 9781101657171.

Gr 3-5–Dyamonde pushes too hard for a new pair of sneakers, so her mom shows her the difference between wants and needs by emptying her closet. When a classmate's family loses everything in a fire, Dyamonde chooses to share much of her wardrobe and discovers that giving to others beats getting new high-tops. Bold, thick line drawings punctuate the text.

Lester, Helen. All for Me and None for All. illus. by Lynn Munsinger. Houghton Mifflin Harcourt. 2012. RTE $16.99. ISBN 9780547688343.
K-Gr 2–Gruntly is a pig in every sense of the word. He even snips the wool and plucks the feathers off the backs of farmyard friends to fluff up his own pillows. At last, though, his greed catches up with him. Written and illustrated with delightfully wry humor, this story of learning how to share will entertain kids and adults alike.

ER O'Connor, Jane. Fancy Nancy: Too Many Tutus. illus. by Robin Preiss Glasser. (I Can Read Series). HarperCollins/Harper. 2013. Tr $16.99. ISBN 9780062083081; pap. $3.99. ISBN 9780062083074; ebk. $4.99. ISBN 9780062083098.

K-Gr 2–Nancy decides to contribute her bounty of tutus to a school swap-and-shop, but it isn't until she lends purchase points to a classmate to help her buy a new tutu they both covet that she truly discovers that giving can be its own gift. With her trademark *joie de vivre*, Nancy shows just how fun sharing can be.

E W Willems, Mo. Should I Share My Ice Cream? illus. by author. (An Elephant and Piggie Book). Hyperion/Disney. 2011. RTE $8.99. ISBN 9781423143437.

PreS-Gr 2–Elephant has a problem: to share or not to share his ice cream with Piggie. With his signature spare style that packs a comedic wallop, Willems encourages readers to laugh as they follow Elephant's humorous, honest crisis of conscience and craving while thinking about what they would do in a similar situation.

BEING HONEST

Dungy, Tony & Lauren Dungy. The Missing Cupcake Mystery. illus. by Vanessa Brantley Newton. (Ready-to-Read Series). S. & S./Spotlight. 2013. Tr $16.99. ISBN 978 144245 4644; pap. $3.99. ISBN 978 1442454637; ebk. $3.99. ISBN 9781 442454651.

K-Gr 2–In this cheerfully illustrated beginning reader featuring a loving family, Jade's mom agrees to buy cupcakes on the condition that they are for after dinner. Yet when it's time for dessert, one of the sweet treats is missing. Jade confesses to eating the cupcake and learns that while disobeying is wrong, telling the truth about it is right.

Giff, Patricia Reilly. Big Whopper. illus. by Alasdair Bright. (Zigzag Kids Series).

Random. 2010. Tr $12.99. ISBN 9780385746885; lib. ed. $15.99. ISBN 9780385909266; pap. $4.99. ISBN 9780553494693; ebk. $4.99. ISBN 9780375896361.

Gr 2-4–Destiny and her classmates are supposed to share a discovery, and desperate to think of something, Destiny claims the first President, "Abraham Washington," is her ancestor. It's a humorous fib but a fib nonetheless, and it causes her great stress. Small, appealing ink images are sprinkled throughout this gentle look at the cost of telling lies.

Jones, Christianne. Hello, Goodbye, and a Very Little Lie. illus. by Christine Battuz. (Little Boost Series). Capstone/Picture Window. 2011. lib. ed. $22.65. ISBN 9781404861671; Tr $7.95. ISBN 9781404874985.

PreS-K–Larry is quite the fibber until a little girl named Lucy calls his bluff. In dire straits, he 'fesses up and gains a friend in the process. Larry's matter-of-fact delivery of his whoppers is hilarious. The characters are charmingly drawn, and the bright, patterned backgrounds complete the appeal.

Martineau, Susan. Being Honest. illus. by Hel James. (Positive Steps Series). Smart Apple Media. 2011. lib. ed. $28.50. ISBN 9781599204895.

Gr 2-4–Cartoon kids mingle with photographed kids in bright, colorful two-page layouts featuring realistic scenarios and questions that teachers and parents can use to encourage children to explore the best ways to handle honesty-related challenges—keeping secrets, making excuses, cheating, and others. Solid nuggets of advice round out the spreads.

PATIENCE, RULES, AND COOPERATION

Alberto, Daisy. No Rules for Rex! illus. by Jerry Smath. (Social Studies Connects Series). Kane. 2005. lib. ed. $15.95. ISBN 9781417687541; pap. $5.95. ISBN 9781575651460.

Gr 1-3–Rex has had enough of rules! His parents suggest a rules-free weekend, but Rex soon realizes life as a free-for-all is not as fun as it sounds. This selection for the just-shy-of-chapter-books crowd combines colorful, funny illustrations with an enjoyable story line and a few factoids about rules in real life to highlight the benefit of boundaries.

Barton, Bethany. This Monster Cannot Wait! illus. by Bethany Barton. Dial. 2013. RTE $16.99. ISBN 9780803737792.

PreS-K–Barton takes a funny look at learning patience through the eyes of Stewart, a snaggle-toothed, green-haired monster who is very excited about an upcoming camping trip. With help from his parents, he finally understands that good things really do come to those who wait. Kids will commiserate and laugh along with Stewart in this very amusing book.

Krulik, Nancy. I Hate Rules! illus. by John & Wendy. (Katie Kazoo, Switcheroo Series: Bk. 5). Grosset & Dunlap. 2003. lib. ed. $13.55. ISBN 9780613602969; pap. $3.99. ISBN 9780448431000; ebk. $3.99. ISBN 9781101098622.

Gr 2-4–Suzanne breaks a rule, but Katie gets punished for it. When a magic wind transforms the third-grader into the school principal, Katie dispenses with all rules, and mayhem ensues. The chaos is fun at first, but ultimately Katie must save Mr. Kane's job. Cute artwork captures the characters throughout.

E
R

Robberecht, Thierry. I Can't Do Anything! tr. from French. illus. by Annick Masson. Magination. 2013. Tr $14.95. ISBN 9781433813092; pap. $9.95. ISBN 9781433813108.

PreS-Gr 1–It's hard to let loose a wild imagination in a world full of rules, but the spunky protagonist recognizes there's a time and a place for almost everything. This engaging story of a frustrated little girl is a great conversation starter about acceptable behavior—if the giggles brought on by the entertaining illustrations don't distract.

Steinkraus, Kyla. Let's Work Together. (Little World Social Skills Series). Rourke. 2012. lib. ed. $24.21. ISBN 9781618101358; pap. $7.95. ISBN 9781618102683.

Gr 1-2–From science lab partners to authors and illustrators, working together is the key to success. The range of examples demonstrating cooperation presented in this title is an effective statement about its importance in the lives of kids and adults. In addition, strategies for working together are offered in kid-friendly terms. Bright photos reinforce the text.

E
Y

Yolen, Jane. How Do Dinosaurs Say I'm Mad? illus. by Mark Teague. Scholastic/Blue Sky. 2013. RTE $16.99. ISBN 9780545143158.

PreS-Gr 2–Giggles will grow with each successive illustration of dinosaurs throwing tantrums in this story about getting mad, which presents a delightful opportunity to talk about appropriate responses when life isn't going your way. After the comical spreads showing mammoth meltdowns, peaceful, helpful advice is offered: take a breath, apologize, and, best of all, give a hug.

DIGITAL PICKS

For Teachers:

Kids for Peace. kidsforpeaceglobal.org/index.php. Kids for Peace, Inc. (Accessed 6/19/14). This is a great website for inspiring and informing efforts to bring about peace through positive participation. Project ideas, a peace pledge, and instructions for starting a local chapter empower kids to become community contributors.

For Students:

It's My Life: Friends. Bullies. pbskids.org/itsmylife/friends/bullies. PBS Kids. (Accessed 6/19/14).

Gr 2-5–Kid-friendly in tone, content, and organization, this informative website defines bullying and offers guidance for dealing with it. The main text is accompanied by a video game that is educational and fun. Peer quotes, additional resources for support, and suggested offline activities are also provided.

Taking Charge of Anger. kidshealth.org/kid/feeling/emotion/anger.html. KidsHealth. (Accessed 6/19/14).

Gr 2-5–There's much useful material here, including a discussion of triggers kids will recognize and a list of "Anger Busters," all delivered in a supportive tone. Links to related topics, for example, "Talking About Your Feelings" and "Train Your Temper,"are provided for those needing additional resources.

Science & Technology

J 53 2 **Adler, David A.** Things That Float and Things That Don't. 32 pp. Holiday 2013. ISBN 978-0-8234-2862-5. Illustrated by Anna Raff.

Adler expertly teaches the concept of density, moving beyond the classic floating and sinking experiments to a carefully constructed lesson that helps young thinkers appreciate both scientific explanations and practices. The concepts are kept simple and age appropriate, without shying away from the more abstract dimensions of science. Cartoonlike illustrations portray two children and their curious dog happily doing science. *Physics and Chemistry; Water; Vehicles—Boats and boating*

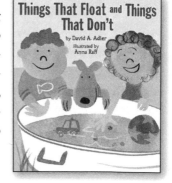

J 63 5 **Ancona, George.** It's Our Garden: From Seeds to Harvest in a School Garden. 48 pp. Candlewick 2013. ISBN 978-0-7636-5392-7. Series.

From spring planting to winterization, full-color photographs chronicle a year in the life of an elementary school garden in Santa Fe; students are shown composting soil, watering plants, and sampling the edible delights. While green is visually ubiquitous, the

real star is the white space, which keeps each spread from becoming crowded. Ancona's no-nonsense text is perfectly suited for newly independent readers. Websites. Bib.
Farm Life/Husbandry/and Gardening; Schools—Elementary schools; New Mexico; Seasons; Composts; Plants; Fruits and vegetables

J

571.455 **Bang, Molly and Chisholm, Penny.** Ocean Sunlight: How Tiny Plants Feed the Seas. 48 pp. Scholastic/Blue Sky (Scholastic Trade Division) 2012. ISBN 978-0-545-27322-0. This fresh perspective on food chains focuses on the critical and voluminous ocean-based plant life—plankton—and the transfer of energy and nutrients from the sun to these microscopic plants to ocean animals and back. Glowing illustrations, age-appropriate explanations, well-chosen text and visual analogies, and a series of rhetorical questions are used to excellent effect. Six pages of notes are appended.
Natural History; Biology; Food chains; Oceans; Astronomy—Sun; Photosynthesis; Plants; Animals—Marine animals

○ **Bishop, Nic.** Nic Bishop Lizards. 48 pp. Scholastic 2010. ISBN 978-0-545-20634-1.
Bishop provides spectacular photographic images, accompanied by excellent scientific information about the many lizard species, their behaviors, anatomy, survival mechanisms, and habitats. Brilliant color photographs bring us sharply into close-ups of the nubby texture of lizard skin or capture frame-by-frame the animals in mid-jump (most impressively across two foldout pages showing every nuance of a basilisk skimming the surface of water). Reading list. Glos., ind.
Reptiles and Amphibians; Animals—Lizards

○ **Bishop, Nic.** Nic Bishop Snakes. 48 pp. Scholastic Nonfiction 2012. ISBN 978-0-545-20638-9.
Seemingly impossible-to-get shots of snakes poised and alert, arched and ready to strike, and even swallowing an egg whole are interspersed with more restful moments during which they are coiled onto branches or camouflaged by sand. It will take a while for readers to tear themselves away from the images to read the excellent accompanying text that describes snake behavior, physiology, and eating habits. Reading list. Glos., ind.
Reptiles and Amphibians; Animals—Snakes

J

641.3 **Butterworth, Chris.** How Did That Get in My Lunchbox?: The Story of Food. 32 pp. Candlewick 2011. ISBN 978-0-7636-5005-6. Illustrated by Lucia Gaggiotti.
This appetizing book encourages readers to think about where food comes from

"before it was in the store." Taking stock of a typical school lunchbox, Butterworth and Gaggiotti serve up an overview of seven familiar ingredients' journeys, shown on well-designed double-page spreads. Butterworth breezily distills the facts down to their essence while Gaggiotti's retro cartoon illustrations are equally informative and appetite-whetting.

Farm Life/Husbandry/and Gardening; Food

Campbell, Eileen. Charlie and Kiwi: An Evolutionary Adventure. 48 pp. Atheneum (Simon & Schuster Children's Publishing) 2011. ISBN 978-1-4424-2112-7. Illustrated by Peter H. Reynolds.

In this age-appropriate, scientifically on-target discussion of evolution, Charlie and his toy-kiwi-come-alive are whisked back in time. They pick up "Grandpa Charles" (a goofy cartoon Darwin) in 1860, then hop back 30 million and 150 million years. At each stop, Grandpa Charles explains individual variation within populations and natural selection. Reynolds's cheery cartoons and the kid-level humor keep the pace and tone upbeat.

Natural History; Scientists; Space and time; Time travel; Animals—Birds; Darwin, Charles; Evolution; Toys

Campbell, Sarah C. Growing Patterns: Fibonacci Numbers in Nature. 32 pp. Boyds 2010. ISBN 978-1-59078-752-6. Photographs by Sarah C. Campbell.

With its glossy, clutter-free pages; crisp, colorful photographs; and clear, straight-to-the-point text, this interactive picture book is an attractive, satisfying introduction to the Fibonacci sequence; a lone seed and a peace lily with its single petal are presented as the first two elements. Photographs of pinecones, pineapples, and sunflowers help demonstrate the concept. "More About Fibonacci Numbers" is appended. Glos.

Mathematics; Nature; Fibonacci, Leonardo; Concept books—Patterns

Chin, Jason. Coral Reefs. 40 pp. Roaring Brook/Flash Point/Porter 2011. ISBN 978-1-59643-563-6.

Chin's text is a straightforward description of corals, their growth into reefs, and interesting inhabitants; his illustrations show a girl in the library pulling out this very book and embarking on an adventure where the contents come to life. Detailed pictures capture the dappled light of shallow water and the bright tropical colors and patterns in the featured flora and fauna.

Natural History; Books and reading; Biomes; Oceans; Coral reefs and islands; Libraries; Animals—Marine animals

Chin, Jason. Island: A Story of the Galápagos. 32 pp. Roaring Brook/Porter 2012. ISBN 978-1-59643-716-6.

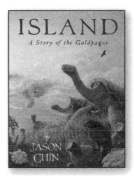

Readers witness the six-million-year development of classic biogeography example of the Galápagos. The organizational structure—five chronological chapters—echoes the story line and underscores the ecological message. Gorgeous illustrations include sweeping double-page spreads and panels arranged to show dynamic changes (e.g., species adaptation). Back matter addresses natural selection, volcano formation/plate tectonics, and endemic species. An author's note discusses scientific facts versus speculation.

General Science and Experiments; Darwin, Charles; Natural disasters—Volcanoes; Evolution; Earth science; Natural history; Galápagos Islands; Islands and island life; Earth science—Plate tectonics

Davies, Nicola. Dolphin Baby! 32 pp. Candlewick 2012. ISBN 978-0-7636-5548-8. Illustrated by Brita Granström.

This lively story of a dolphin baby and his caring mother is infused with scientific details about dolphin developmental milestones in the first six months of life. While the main narrative concentrates on one particular dolphin as he matures, smaller text on each spread provides more general information about the species. A touch anthropomorphized, the illustrations do convey dolphins' high intelligence. Ind.

Mammals; Animal babies; Life cycles; Animals—Dolphins; Animals—Marine animals

Fern, Tracey. Barnum's Bones: How Barnum Brown Discovered the Most Famous Dinosaur in the World. 40 pp. Farrar/Ferguson 2012. ISBN 978-0-374-30516-1. Illustrated by Boris Kulikov.

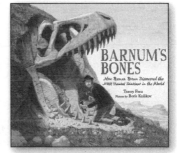

Barnum Brown was an eccentric dinosaur hunter who, at and around the turn of the last century, amassed a peerless collection of fossilized skeletons for the American Museum of Natural History in New York City. The colorful narrative bubbles with Barnum's irrepressible fervor; bright, saturated

paintings bring the landscapes of the cultured city and Wild West to vivid life. Bib.
Prehistoric Life; Biographies; Prehistoric life—Dinosaurs; Fossils; Brown, Barnum; Paleontology; Museums

George, Jean Craighead. Galápagos George. 40 pp. HarperCollins/Harper 2014. ISBN 978-0-06-028793-1. Illustrated by Wendell Minor.

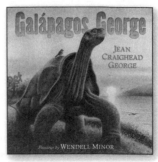

The author asks readers to extrapolate from the life cycle of a single female Galápagos tortoise, Giantess George, to the development of the species as a whole. She and other tortoises are swept away to different islands in a storm; over thousands of years, they evolve into different subspecies. Minor's painterly illustrations showcase the changing setting and the magnificence of the tortoises. Reading list, timeline, websites. Glos.
Reptiles and Amphibians; Galápagos Islands; Animals—Tortoises; Evolution

Huber, Raymond. Flight of the Honey Bee. 32 pp. Candlewick 2013. ISBN 978-0-7636-6760-3. Illustrated by Brian Lovelock.

As the hive prepares for winter, worker bee Scout embarks on a food-foraging expedition, searching for enough nectar and pollen to survive. Huber's simple but dynamic language hums with an avian vibrancy. In Lovelock's watercolor, acrylic ink, and colored-pencil illustrations, splattered dots represent pollen and hailstones; textured brushstrokes convey flight patterns, vibrating wings, and pelting rain. A satisfying early science book. Ind.
Insects and Invertebrates; Animals—Bees; Animals—Honeybees

Jenkins, Steve. The Beetle Book. 40 pp. Houghton (Houghton Mifflin Trade and Reference Division) 2012. ISBN 978-0-547-68084-2.

Highlighting the amazing diversity of this truly fascinating insect order, the book opens with basic beetle structure and function and then covers topics such as reproduction, feeding, communication, and defense mechanisms. Jenkins's colorful cut-paper illustrations are remarkably detailed, and the to-scale silhouettes found on the bottom of many spreads provide very helpful information on the range of beetle sizes.
Insects and Invertebrates; Animals—Beetles

J
573.76

Jenkins, Steve. Bones: Skeletons and How They Work. 48 pp. Scholastic 2010. ISBN 978-0-545-04651-0.

Bones of all shapes and sizes glow like jewels on richly colored backgrounds, allowing readers to pore over every nuance of Jenkins's intricate cut-paper illustrations. The discussion smartly begins with human anatomy; page turns reveal a comparative presentation of five other animals. Foldouts allow python and human skeletons to be introduced in even finer detail. Quirky bone facts are appended.
Medicine/Human Body/and Diseases; Human body—Skeletal system; Bones; Toy and mov able books

E
J

Judge, Lita. Bird Talk: What Birds Are Saying and Why. 48 pp. Roaring Brook/Flash Point 2012. ISBN 978-1-59643-646-6.

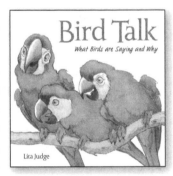

Judge explains the ways in which birds communicate, and the reasons why they do so, with examples selected from a variety of bird species. The striking illustrations deftly portray communication as a whole-body endeavor, capturing the expressions, movements, and positions at key points in the messages that birds send within and across species. Additional facts about each species are appended. Bib., glos.
Birds; Animal communication

J
567.9

Judge, Lita. Born to Be Giants: How Baby Dinosaurs Grew to Rule the World. 48 pp. Roaring Brook/Flash Point 2010. ISBN 978-1-59643-443-1.

Judge explains the birth and care of dinosaur young. The text is a model of logical reasoning: each claim is backed by relevant evidence. Although much of what is presented is speculation, it's speculation grounded in the best scientific research. The detailed, richly colored illustrations, which often place readers at baby-dinosaur eye level, take the same care in balancing accuracy and imagination. Timeline. Bib., glos.
Prehistoric Life; Prehistoric life—Dinosaurs; Animal babies

Q

Judge, Lita. How Big Were Dinosaurs? 40 pp. Roaring Brook 2013. ISBN 978-1-59643-719-7.

Dinosaurs came in a range of shapes and sizes. Judge helps us understand the variations in size by creatively placing dinosaurs in juxtaposition with familiar modern-day animals and objects. Both illustrations (in pencil and watercolor wash) and descriptions draw on the familiar: Protoceratops sidles up to a baby rhinoceros; Ankylosaurus menaces an SUV. A foldout contains a to-scale illustration of all the dinosaurs together. Reading list, websites.

Prehistoric life—Dinosaurs

E
L
Leedy, Loreen. Seeing Symmetry. 32 pp. Holiday 2012. ISBN 978-0-8234-2360-6.
Leedy points out that "if you can fold a shape exactly in half, it has symmetry." Her many visual examples, complete with the imaginary line of symmetry drawn in, will help young math students understand the concept. The pages are colorful, lively, and easy to understand in this encouraging, accurate book. Suggested activities and further explanations extend the text. Glos.

Mathematics; Mathematics—Symmetry; Mathematics—Ratios

also   J 516.1

O
Lewin, Ted and Lewin, Betsy. Puffling Patrol. 56 pp. Lee 2012. ISBN 978-1-60060-424-9.
Fledgling puffins journeying from their nests to the sea are confused by nighttime lights from towns. In Iceland, on the island of Heimaey, children take part in a generations-old puffin search-and-rescue tradition. As they tour the island with researchers, then join a night patrol, the Lewins capture the beauty of the landscape and the awkwardly amusing appeal of the birds.

Birds; Animals—Puffins; Animal babies; Wildlife rescue; Islands and island life; Iceland

O
Lunde, Darrin. After the Kill. 32 pp. Charlesbridge 2011. ISBN 978-1-57091-743-1. PE ISBN 978-1-57091-744-8. Illustrated by Catherine Stock.
In this blunt portrayal of animal life in the Serengeti, a lioness stalks and kills a zebra. Vultures, hyenas, jackals, and meat-eating beetles arrive until all that remains of the zebra is bones. Given the topic's inherent grisliness, the text is notably matter-of-fact. The pictures, expansive horizontal spreads, are almost impressionistic, focusing more on the predators' ferocity than details of their prey.

Natural History; Animal behavior; Animals—Lions; Food chains

J
629.133
Macaulay, David. Jet Plane: How It Works. 32 pp. Square Fish/David Macaulay Studio 2012. ISBN 978-1-59643-764-7. PE ISBN 978-1-59643-767-8. My Readers series. With Sheila Keenan.
Macaulay brings his signature brand of illustrated expository nonfiction to a

younger audience. This book revisits a subject Macaulay has written about previously, but the topics are here presented with the needs of developing readers in mind. Notable for the amount of technical details packed into thirty-two pages, the narrative invites readers to envision themselves in the action; words and pictures effectively weave information into this framework. Reading list, websites. Glos., ind.

Machines and Technology; Vehicles—Airplanes; Flight

○ **Macaulay, David.** Toilet: How It Works. 32 pp. Square Fish/David Macaulay Studio 2013. ISBN 978-1-59643-779-1. PE ISBN 978-1-59643-780-7. Other by Sheila Keenan. My Readers series.

In this beginning reader/nonfiction chapter book, clear step-by-step directions and unobstructed diagrams and cross sections outline how waste is produced by the body, disposed of through a toilet, sent to either a septic tank or sewer system, and purified. Macaulay's humor is evident, as he reminds readers that the language of science can be both precise and lively. Reading list, websites. Glos., ind.

Machines and Technology; Hygiene

○ **Markle, Sandra.** The Long, Long Journey: The Godwit's Amazing Migration. 40 pp. Millbrook 2013. LE ISBN 978-0-7613-5623-3. Illustrated by Mia Posada.

The bar-tailed godwit is a shorebird with residences in Alaska and New Zealand. Brief text conveys information about godwit behaviors as they learn to fly, forage, and eat the enormous amount of food needed to fuel the journey. Creative paper-collage illustrations capture the fuzzy down of newborn chicks and the starry nights of flying. A list of resources is provided.

Birds; Migration

○ **Martin, Jacqueline Briggs.** The Chiru of High Tibet: A True Story. 40 pp. Houghton (Houghton Mifflin Trade and Reference Division) 2010. ISBN 978-0-618-58130-6. Illustrated by Linda Wingerter.

The antelope-like chiru of northern Tibet were hunted nearly to extinction for their soft wool. Wildlife champion George Schaller hoped to save the chiru by protecting their birthing ground—but first he had to find it. Martin's account, brief and dramatic, is nicely amplified in Wingerter's art, evoking Tibet's windswept plains and peaks in rosy sunset colors and twilight blues. Bib.

Mammals; Environment—Endangered species; Mountains and mountain life; Wildlife rescue; Environment—Conservation—Wildlife

E
Mc

McCarthy, Meghan. Pop!: The Invention of Bubble Gum. 40 pp. Simon/Wiseman 2010. ISBN 978-1-4169-7970-8.

In 1928 mild-mannered accountant/inventor Walter Diemer introduced bubble gum to the American public. This light-as-air biography covers a popular topic and a likable hero whose success comes through hard work, perseverance, and ingenuity. McCarthy's signature round-faced characters, with spherical insectlike eyes, suggest gumballs playfully rolling across each page. An author's note including interesting facts about chewing gum continues the good-humored theme. Bib.

Machines and Technology; Inventions and inventors; Candy; Diemer, Walter; Biographies

E
M

McCully, Emily Arnold. Wonder Horse: The True Story of the World's Smartest Horse. 32 pp. Holt 2010. ISBN 978-0-8050-8793-2.

Bill "Doc" Key, born a slave, later became a veterinarian. Apparently, Doc taught his astonishingly intelligent horse, Jim Key, the alphabet, numbers, even colors. In her concluding note, McCully is suitably skeptical; but whatever truths lie behind this engaging tale, it's a fine portrait of accomplishment. In McCully's signature watercolors, the pre-industrial setting and its rural inhabitants are realized at their bucolic best. Bib.

Domestic Animals; Biographies; Key, Bill; African Americans; Animals—Horses; Veterinarians; Slavery

O

Munro, Roxie. Busy Builders. 40 pp. Cavendish (Marshall Cavendish Corp.) 2012. ISBN 978-0-7614-6105-0.

Profiles of eight insects (and one spider) that make their own structures are presented. Each is introduced with a wonderfully close-up illustration and the question, "Where does it live?" Turn the page to see the organisms industriously building and maintaining their home. Detailed explanations on the construction techniques and purposes of the structures are interwoven with facts about each species' life cycles. Bib., glos.

Insects and Invertebrates; Animal behavior; Animal homes

O

Munro, Roxie. Hatch! 40 pp. Cavendish (Marshall Cavendish Corp.) 2011. ISBN 978-0-7614-5882-1.

In an engaging guessing-game format, Munro presents fascinating fact-profiles of nine mostly familiar birds. Each double-page spread shows an egg close-up with clues about its producer; turn the page to find the answer as well as Munro's colorful, detailed illustrations of nesting habitats. A helpful list of the other animals in the illustrations encourages even more interactivity. Reading list, websites. Glos.

Birds; Animal babies; Eggs; Questions and answers

Newman, Mark. Polar Bears. 32 pp. Holt 2010. ISBN 978-0-8050-8999-8.

Irresistibly endearing polar bear photographs—numerous icy-blue pictures of adults and babies in their natural habitats—are the highlight of this memorable book. Each spread includes a genuinely interesting factual statement about polar bears accompanied by smaller additional text that goes into deeper detail. In the final sections, Newman emphasizes the challenges polar bears face due to climate change. Websites.

Mammals; Animals—Polar bears; Environment—Conservation—Wildlife

J
99.674   **O'Connell, Caitlin.** A Baby Elephant in the Wild. 40 pp. Houghton (Houghton Mifflin Trade and Reference Division) 2014. ISBN 978-0-544-14944-1. Photographs by Caitlin O'Connell.

In text and numerous color photographs we follow a newborn female elephant through her first months in the Namibian scrub desert as she learns the behaviors that will enable her to survive. The account is straightforward and unsentimental yet filled with detailed and fascinating scientific information, including the lifelong ties among elephants that will resonate with readers' own experience of family.

Mammals; Namibia; Africa; Animal babies; Animals—Elephants; Savannas

Peterson, Brenda. Leopard & Silkie: One Boy's Quest to Save the Seal Pups. 32 pp. Holt/Ottaviano 2012. ISBN 978-0-8050-9167-0. Photographs by Robin Lindsey. series.

The Seal Sitters is a Pacific Northwest watch group that educates human beachgoers and protects harbor seals when they come ashore to give birth to and care for their young. Newborn seal Leopard is fortunate to have "kid volunteer" Miles on the case. In the excellent photographs, Leopard's large, dark eyes and expressive mug seem to be smiling right at the viewer.

Mammals; Animals—Seals; Wildlife rescue; Environment—Conservation—Wildlife; Children

Pfeffer, Wendy. Light Is All Around Us. 40 pp. HarperCollins/Harper 2014. ISBN 978-0-06-029121-1. PE ISBN 978-0-06-440924-7. Illustrated by Paul Meisel. Let's-Read-and-Find-Out Science series.

This strong series entry introduces youngsters to light: where it comes from, how fast it travels, and how it enables us to see. The prose is generally lively, but Pfeffer is all business when it comes to scientific explanations. Lighthearted paintings, outlined in pen and ink, add humor but never distract from the text. Three simple experiments are appended.

Physics and Chemistry; Light

E
P
Potter, Alicia. Mrs. Harkness and the Panda. 40 pp. Knopf (Random House Children's Books) 2012. ISBN 978-0-375-84448-5. LE ISBN 978-0-375-94448-2. Illustrated by Melissa Sweet.

Ruth Harkness, newly widowed, set out in 1936 to complete her husband's mission: to fetch what would be the first-ever panda from China. Her return to America with a young panda was a triumph. The engaging narrative is illustrated with delicate watercolors enriched with collages of Chinese fabrics, maps, postcards, and more to evoke period, place, and dramatic action. Bib.

Mammals; Harkness, Ruth; Animals—Pandas; China; Voyages and travels

C
Preus, Margi. Celebritrees: Historic and Famous Trees of the World. 40 pp. Holt/Ottaviano 2011. ISBN 978-0-8050-7829-9. Illustrated by Rebecca Gibbon.

This picture book gallery of impressive trees, illustrated in friendly folk-art style, offers substantive information on what makes each specimen unique. Preus discusses world-record holders as well as fascinating oddities; a number of the trees have cultural significance. Gibbon's mixed-media paintings bustle with life, including birds and squirrels in the high branches and people in the shade. Conservation tips are appended. Websites. Bib.

Botany; Trees; Environment—Conservation—Natural resources

E
P
Provensen, Alice and Provensen, Martin. The Glorious Flight: Across the Channel with Louis Blériot. 40 pp. Viking 2010. ISBN 978-0-670-34259-4. Reissue, 1983.

The Provensens' sublime picture book (winner of the 1984 Caldecott Medal) about French aviation pioneer Louis Blériot, the first man to fly across the English Channel, is once again available in hardcover. With breathtaking perspectives, gorgeous colors, engaging characters, and a *très* droll text, the book not only transports readers to turn-of-the-twentieth-century France but also conveys the experience of flight with immediacy.

Machines and Technology; Flight; Vehicles—Airplanes; Blériot, Louis; Pilots

(Caldecott 1984)

J
530.B

Robbins, Ken. For Good Measure: The Ways We Say How Much, How Far, How Heavy, How Big, How Old. 48 pp. Roaring Brook/Flash Point/Porter 2010. ISBN 978-1-59643-344-1.

Robbins's picture book photo essay is a multi-layered investigation of standard units of measurement—their definitions, purposes, origins, contexts, and histories. Clear and well-organized, the text is invitingly conversational and chock-full of interesting tidbits. Photographs go beyond informative to arresting: there's a photo of a stone that's so crisp you can almost feel its warmth and texture.

Mathematics; Mathematics—Measurement

Root, Phyllis. Big Belching Bog. 40 pp. Minnesota 2010. ISBN 978-0-8166-3359-3. Illustrated by Betsy Bowen.

This book invites readers into the stillness of a northern Minnesota bog. Root's prose conveys the mellow characteristics and funkiness of the bog, while Bowen's stylized woodcut illustrations, predominantly black, blue, purple, and green, capture the murky but nonetheless teeming-with-life place. The book ends with further factual information about these fascinating and eerie natural environments.

Natural History; Biomes; Animals; Habitats; Nature; Minnesota; Wetlands

Roth, Susan L. and Cindy Trumbore. Parrots over Puerto Rico. 48 pp. Lee 2013. ISBN 978-1-62014-004-8. Illustrated by Susan L. Roth.

This gorgeously illustrated history of the endangered Puerto Rican parrot underscores the environmental consequences of human populations on indigenous animal species. With stunning paper-and-fabric artwork, the book is laid out vertically to give a sense of height. Ruffly-feathered parrots, colorfully clothed people, and Puerto Rican landmarks are located within dense, intricate illustrations that capture the lushness of the landscape. Timeline.

Animals—Parrots; Puerto Rico; Environment—Endangered species; Environment—Conservation—Wildlife

Rumford, James. From the Good Mountain: How Gutenberg Changed the World. 40 pp. Roaring Brook/Flash Point/Porter 2012. ISBN 978-1-59643-542-1. series.

In this inviting very-first look at Gutenberg's transformative invention and the intricate craft of early printing, Rumford vivifies the ways and means of medieval innovation with intriguing details, focusing on highlights. An epilogue elucidates and extends the occasionally too-truncated information, as does handsome watercolor and gouache art that recalls illuminated manuscripts while revealing additional tasks, hazards, and sources of inspiration.

Machines and Technology; Gutenberg, Johann; Printing; Books and reading; Germany

Rusch, Elizabeth. Volcano Rising. 32 pp. Charlesbridge 2013. ISBN 978-1-58089-408-1. PE ISBN 978-1-58089-409-8. Illustrated by Susan Swan.

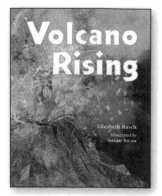

The book opens with a magnificent mixed-media illustration showing a volcanic vent gushing steam, rock, and lava. The author then confronts a common misconception: "Volcanoes are not just destructive. Much more often, volcanoes are creative." Profiles of eight volcanoes illustrate her point. Each spread includes one sentence in large type that provides general information; smaller-type paragraphs provide detailed background. Reading list. Bib., glos.

Earth Science; Natural disasters—Volcanoes

Sayre, April Pulley. Eat like a Bear. 32 pp. Holt 2013. ISBN 978-0-8050-9039-0. Illustrated by Steve Jenkins.

In a comfortingly repetitive, cadenced text ("Can you hunt like a bear? / It's June. Find food. / But where?"), direct questions ask readers not only if they can eat but also search, gather, climb, and even bathe like a brown bear. Jenkins's torn-paper illustrations are reproduced with such clarity that one can almost grasp the thick, fuzzy fur of the bear.

Mammals; Animals—Bears; Stories in rhyme

Sayre, April Pulley. Turtle, Turtle, Watch Out! 32 pp. Charlesbridge 2010. ISBN 978-1-58089-148-6. PE ISBN 978-1-58089-149-3. Illustrated by Annie Patterson. New ed., 2000, Orchard.

Very few sea turtles survive to adulthood. This book's turtle is one of the fortunate ones, thanks to the assistance of volunteers who protect turtle nests and keep hatchlings safe. Readers will be drawn in by Turtle's newborn awkwardness, captured adroitly by Patterson's new softly colored realistic illustrations, and will rally to the cause through the text's repeated use of the title warning.

Reptiles and Amphibians; Animals—Sea turtles; Wildlife rescue; Animals—Turtles; Environment—Endangered species

E
S

Schaefer, Lola M. Lifetime: The Amazing Numbers in Animal Lives. 40 pp. Chronicle 2013. ISBN 978-1-4521-0714-1. Illustrated by Christopher Silas Neal.

The concept of quantity is cleverly examined in the context of animal lives. Schaefer presents the number of times an animal "performs one behavior" in its lifetime, starting with the single egg sac spun by a spider, up to the thousand babies carried by a male seahorse. Bold and beautifully composed, Neal's retro illustrations contain the actual number of items mentioned. Supplemental information is appended.
Animals; Biology

Ⓠ **Simon, Seymour.** Butterflies. 32 pp. HarperCollins/Collins (HarperCollins) 2011. ISBN 978-0-06-191493-5.

Simon begins his clear and friendly explanations with the monarch butterfly and its remarkable migration. He then moves to a more general discussion of moth and butterfly life cycles, structure and function, species similarities and variations, and importance to humans. The outstanding full-page color photographs are perfectly in sync with the text, with each focused sharply on the pertinent details. Glos., ind.
Insects and Invertebrates; Animals—Butterflies; Animals—Moths

Ⓠ **Spinner, Stephanie.** Alex the Parrot: No Ordinary Bird. 40 pp. Knopf (Random House Children's Books) 2012. ISBN 978-0-375-86846-7. LE ISBN 978-0-375-96846-4. Illustrated by Meilo So. series.

In her groundbreaking studies with African grey parrot Alex (acronym for "Avian Learning Experiment"), Irene Pepperberg successfully teaches him language skills beyond the usual mimicry. Spinner explains methods clearly and dynamically, but readers will most enjoy displays of Alex's personality. So's mixed-media illustrations, with their agile lines and splashes of tropical color against white backgrounds, further enliven the text's details.
Birds; Animals—Parrots; Experiments; Animal behavior; Animal communication

J
641.3

Stewart, Melissa and Allen Young. No Monkeys, No Chocolate. 32 pp. Charlesbridge 2013. ISBN 978-1-58089-287-2. Illustrated by Nicole Wong.

Stewart and Young explain where chocolate comes from: working backward from cocoa beans (dried and processed by humans) to cocoa pods (which come from cocoa flowers pollinated by midges) to monkeys dropping cocoa seeds on the rainforest floor. Full-bleed ink and watercolor illustrations zoom in on each step along the way; in a corner of each spread, two little worms provide humorous running commentary.

Biodiversity; Plants; Rainforests

Yezerski, Thomas F. Meadowlands: A Wetlands Survival Story. 40 pp. Farrar 2011. ISBN 978-0-374-34913-4.

Yezerski adroitly captures the sometimes adversarial, sometimes beneficial relationship between humans and the environment in this marvelous ecological history of the Meadowlands of New Jersey. Each main double-page-spread illustration is bordered by tiny images with a wealth of additional taxonomical information (and sly humor) about the diverse flora and fauna (and mobsters and sports enthusiasts) of northern New Jersey. Websites. Bib.

Natural History; Environment—Conservation; Wetlands; New Jersey; Environment—Ecology

E
Z

Zoehfeld, Kathleen Weidner. Secrets of the Garden: Food Chains and the Food Web in Our Backyard. 40 pp. Knopf (Random House Children's Books) 2012. ISBN 978-0-517-70990-0. Illustrated by Priscilla Lamont.
Alice and her family grow edible plants, raise chickens, and enjoy the wide variety of living things in their backyard ecosystem. Scientific information is included about such topics as

composting, plant life cycles, food chains and food webs, and nutrition, with anthropomorphized chickens explaining the underlying facts. Changes during the garden growing season are attractively portrayed in Lamont's cheery illustrations.

Farm Life/Husbandry/and Gardening; Life cycles; Plants; Food chains; Animals—Chickens

Zoehfeld, Kathleen Weidner. Where Did Dinosaurs Come From? 40 pp. HarperCollins/ Collins (HarperCollins) 2011. ISBN 978-0-06-029022-1. PE ISBN 978-0-06-445216-8. Illustrated by Lucia Washburn. Let's-Read-and-Find-Out Science series. After a brief introduction, the book concentrates on the period from 330 million years ago to 65 million years ago, from the appearance of amniotes through the myriad dinosaur species that thrived in the Mesozoic Era. Zoehfeld is remarkably precise with language, providing outstanding explanations of key concepts. Wash-

burn's illustrations include helpful anatomical details and imagined portrayals of dinosaurs in verdant habitats. Timeline. Glos.
Prehistoric Life; Prehistoric life—Dinosaurs

. . . .

—FOCUS ON—
Healthy Lifestyles
A Balancing Act
By Joanna K. Fabicon

Joanna K. Fabicon is a Children's Librarian at Los Angeles Public Library, CA.

. . . .

It seems as though not a day goes by without the media covering a story about children's health. Fast-food restaurants decide to list the nutritional information of their entrees. School districts ban soft-drink vending machines in their cafeterias. Childhood obesity is at epidemic levels. Affecting everyone is the recent Supreme Court decision on healthcare reform. The downside to all the attention is shading the notion of health with alarmist, prohibitive, or political attitudes. Getting children interested in the topic may be as hard as getting them to eat vegetables. The following titles for preschool through teen readers find the joy in being healthy, whether through realistic voices or characters, empowering youth to make their own choices, revealing fascinating facts about what goes on underneath our skin, or encouraging readers to lead active lives. Here's to reading for health!

THINKING ABOUT HEALTH

Bunting, Eve. My Dog Jack Is Fat. illus. by Michael Rex. Marshall Cavendish. 2011. RTE $16.99. ISBN 978-0-7614-5809-8.
K-Gr 1–Exercise and smaller portions are on the menu after the vet determines that Carson's dog, Jack, is overweight. But as Jack struggles on a treadmill, Carson snacks on junk food. Comic illustrations anticipate the role reversal at Jack's next appointment when the vet gently advises Carson to try "a little bit of what Jack's been doing."

J
641.3

Butterworth, Christine. How Did That Get in My Lunchbox? The Story of Food. illus. by Lucia Gaggiotti. Candlewick. 2011. Tr $12.99. ISBN 978-0-7636-5005-6.

PreS-Gr 2–Retro-style cartoon illustrations and an engaging text follow the production of common edibles so the younger set can see where the food in a typical lunchbox comes from. Gaggiotti's rendition of MyPlate (a new USDA nutrition guide) and a page of food facts reveal that lunch is just one component in a full day of healthy eating.

C

Campbell, Bebe Moore. I Get So Hungry. illus. by Amy Bates. Putnam. 2008. RTE $16.99. ISBN 978-0-399-24311-0.

K-Gr 3–Though Nikki knows it's wrong to find comfort in junk food, her mother's unhealthy eating habits offer uneasy validation. After a medical scare, Nikki's overweight teacher begins to turn things around by eating better and walking around the school every morning; Nikki decides to join her. Watercolor scenes add to this sensitive and thoughtful story.

E
C

Child, Lauren. I Will Never Not Ever Eat a Tomato. illus. by author. Candlewick. 2000. RTE $15.99. ISBN 978-0-76-361188-0.

PreS-Gr 2–Carrots become "orange twiglets from Jupiter" and mashed potatoes are made of cloud fluff from Mount Fuji as the enduring Charlie convinces his picky, younger sister, Lola, to eat her dinner. Kids and parents will appreciate Charlie's creative approach to vegetables while humorous mixed-media art adds to the fun.

C

Cobb, Vicki. Your Body Battles a Stomachache. photomicrographs by Dennis Kunkel. illus. by Andrew N. Harris. (Body Battlefields Series). Millbrook. 2009. PLB $25.26. ISBN 978-0-8225-7166-7.

Gr 1-4–Cells magnified by a scanning electron microscope combine with superhero illustrations and conversational text to provide a complete picture of how our bodies rally to fight off a variety of infections and injuries. Though the focus is on healing and not overall health, there are hints scattered throughout. Other titles in the series are equally engaging.

E
C

Corey, Shana. Mermaid Queen: The Spectacular True Story of Annette Kellerman, Who Swam Her Way to Fame, Fortune, and Swimsuit History! illus. by Edwin Fotheringham. Scholastic. 2009. Tr $17.99. ISBN 978-0-439-69835-1.

Gr 2-5–Born in 1886, this inventor of water ballet and the modern swimsuit broke down barriers in both sports and fashion and "believed exercise was key not just to health but to self-esteem." Bright digital-media illustrations evoke the period and capture Kellerman's zest and grace. Those looking for a role model will find an incredible one here.

○ **Gutman, Dan.** Ms. Leakey Is Freaky! illus. by Jim Paillot. (My Weird School Daze Series). HarperCollins. 2011. PLB $15.89. ISBN 978-0-06-170403-1.
Gr 3-5–An overzealous health teacher will stop at nothing to get her students to eat right, even if it means ambushing them at the grocery store. Admonishments like, "Do you know what they put in a 3 Musketeers bar?" could prompt readers to take a look at nutritional labels. Zany cartoons packed with kid-appeal are interspersed.

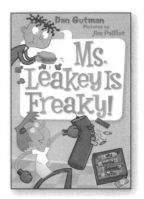

○ **Harper, Charise Mericle.** Henry's Heart: A Boy, His Heart, and a New Best Friend. illus. by author. Holt/Christy Ottaviano Bks. 2011. RTE $16.99. ISBN 978-0-8050-8989-9.
K-Gr 3–Genially drawn with its own eyes and mouth, Henry's heart beats in response to emotional and physical changes. Information about circulation and heart-friendly foods gets woven into the story of Henry's wanting a new puppy, making it easy for children to learn how to make their own hearts happy (and healthy).

○ **McCarthy, Meghan.** Strong Man: The Story of Charles Atlas. illus. by author. Knopf. 2007. Tr $15.99. ISBN 978-0-375-82940-6; PLB $18.99. ISBN 978-0-375-92940-3.
Gr 1-5–Tormented by bullies, skinny Angelo Siciliano developed his own fitness routine and eventually became Charles Atlas, "The World's Most Perfectly Developed Man." Just as Atlas gained millions of young fans in his time, today's readers will be inspired by his determination and commitment to health in this picture-book biography boasting colorful cartoon illustrations.

E
R　**Rockwell, Lizzy.** The Busy Body Book: A Kid's Guide to Fitness. illus. by author. Crown. 2004. Tr $15.95. ISBN 978-0-37-582203-2; PLB $17.99. ISBN 978-0-37-592203-9.
PreS-Gr 3–Cheerful illustrations of active children in a park are followed by a

diagram of a skeleton. The simple format repeats with muscles, the brain and nerves, lungs, heart and blood vessels, and the stomach and intestines. While providing a vocabulary for body parts, the book relays the connection between exercise and a healthy body.

GET UP AND MOVE

Cronin, Doreen. Stretch. illus. by Scott Menchin. S & S/Atheneum. 2009. RTE $15.99. ISBN 978-1-4169-5341-8.

PreS-K–When creating a workout routine from Cronin and Menchin's collaborations, it's best to start with *Stretch before Wiggle* (2005) and *Bounce* (2007). After all, stretching can be done anywhere, even with imagined animals. All three titles sport an appealingly active canine energized by brightly colored pen-and-ink drawings. Use as wiggle-relieving openers before starting class or at storytime.

Go Out and Play! Favorite Outdoor Games from KaBOOM! illus. by Juliana Rose. Candlewick. 2012. pap. $11.99. ISBN 978-0-7636-5530-3.

K Up–With just over 70 activities for outside play, children and parents will find the classics (from hide-and-seek to Duck, Duck, Goose) mixed in with creative variations on tag, relay races, and other games. Each page features one game explained with concise playing instructions and other requirements. Sections on facilitating play and getting involved ensure fun for all ages.

Spinelli, Eileen. Miss Fox's Class Shapes Up. illus. by Anne Kennedy. Albert Whitman. 2011. Tr $16.99. ISBN 978-0-8075-5171-4.

K-Gr 2–When her breakfast-skipping, low-energy students fall asleep at their desks, Miss Fox decides that becoming fit is a priority. The school nurse offers nutritious recipes; recess brings experimentation with jump ropes and Hula-Hoops, and cheerfully active animal characters demonstrate that being healthy is its own reward. Includes easy-to-adopt health and fitness tips.

Thompson, Lauren. Hop, Hop, Jump! illus. by Jarrett J. Krosoczka. S & S/Margaret K. McElderry Bks. 2012. Tr $14.99. ISBN 978-1-4169-9745-0.

PreS-K–Children in a summer-camp setting enthusiastically demonstrate how to move different body parts, be it a finger ("Wiggle it."), toe ("Waggle it."), or bottom and head ("Upside-down it."). A simple text and acrylic cartoon drawings sporting smiling boys and girls jumping, swimming, and enjoying the outdoors produce a lively storytime addition.

Ⓠ **Yoo, Taeeun. You Are a Lion! And Other Fun Yoga Poses.** illus. by author. Penguin/ Nancy Paulsen Bks. 2012. RTE $16.99. ISBN 978-0-399-25602-8.

PreS-Gr 2–Opening with a lovely, artistic rendition of a sun salutation, six multicultural children meet in a forest clearing to greet the morning with yoga stretches. The following pages show each child demonstrating a single age-appropriate pose (dog, mountain, lion, etc.), complemented by easy-to-imitate instructions. Yoo has crafted a perfect introduction to the practice.

EATING HEALTHY AND DELICIOUS FOOD

J
635.

Gibbons, Gail. The Vegetables We Eat. illus. by author. Holiday House. 2007. RTE $16.95. ISBN 978-0-8234-2001-8.

K-Gr 4–Eager learners will find vegetable facts galore in this vibrant introduction, illustrated in Gibbons's signature style. Topics such as the eight different kinds of vegetables (with more than fifty varieties presented), the journey from the farm to store, and how to create your own garden are sure to nourish interest and eating.

E
G

Gourley, Robbin. First Garden: The White House Garden and How It Grew. illus. by author. Clarion. 2011. Tr $16.99. ISBN 978-0-547-48224-8.

K-Gr 4–Gourley includes an historical perspective in this engaging title, but the heart of the matter is the effort spearheaded by Michelle Obama, who recruited local elementary school children to help plant the current garden. The garden's success story, effectively paired with vibrant watercolor illustrations, champions home gardening and local produce as important aspects of healthy eating and living.

Ⓠ **Grow It, Cook It: Simple Gardening Projects and Delicious Recipes.** DK. 2008. Tr $15.99. ISBN 978-0-75-663367-7.

Gr 3-6–After a brief overview of plants, recycling and compost, and a list of cooking terms, hands-on gardening and cooking begins with pictures accompanying each step of the instructions. Related recipes follow the featured vegetable, fruit, or herb (pumpkin, carrots, spinach, strawberries, to name a few) and encourage children to take ownership of healthy food choices.

Ⓠ **Iwai, Melissa. Soup Day.** illus. by author. Holt/Christy Ottaviano Bks. 2010. Tr $12.99. ISBN 978-0-8050-9004-8.

PreS-Gr 2–Healthy habits abound in this simple story about a girl and her mother making soup on a snowy winter day. They walk to the market, choose the freshest vegetables, chop the ingredients together, and stay active as the pot simmers.

Charming collage illustrations capture the warmth while a Snowy Day Vegetable Soup recipe provides inspiration.

E
S **Sayre, April Pulley.** Go, Go, Grapes!: A Fruit Chant. 2012. Tr $16.99. ISBN 978-1-44-243390-8.
----. Rah, Rah, Radishes!: A Vegetable Chant. 2011. Tr $15.99. ISBN 978-1-4424-2141-7.

ea vol: photos by author. S & S/Beach Lane. PreS-Gr 1–The infectiously joyful cadence of the chants and the enticingly photographed fruits and vegetables guarantee bouncing and clapping along with probable demands for repeated readings (and possibly trips to the nearest farmer's market). While featuring the ubiquitous (carrots, corn, apples), Sayre's paeans to produce also capture the deliciously unfamiliar (kohlrabi, rambutan, mangosteen), and might be the first step to children's healthy eating.

MEDIA PICKS
By Phyllis Levy Mandell

Achoo! Stop the Flu. DVD. 30 min. Prod. by Rolling River Prods. Dist. by TMW Media Group. 2011. ISBN unavail. $64.95.
K-Gr 6–How can you stay healthy during flu season? The Grammy award-winning folk group The Kingston Trio, along with Julie Thompson and Brownie Macintosh (The Julie and Brownie Show), offer suggestions via skits and five catchy sing-along tunes. They encourage washing hands, staying hydrated, getting rest, exercising, and eating a healthy diet.

Healthy Food for Thought: Good Enough to Eat. 2 CDs. approx. 2 hrs. Prod. by East Coast Record Co. Dist. by healthyfoodforthought.com. 2010. $10 (+ $3 s/h).
PreS-Gr 4–This compilation, nominated for a Grammy award for best spoken word album, consists of 60 selections of prose, poems, and songs provided by kids' musicians and authors about food, nutrition, and self-awareness that can be used as part of a childhood obesity awareness curriculum.

MyPlate and You: Learning About Nutrition, Health, and Exercise. DVD. 16 min. with tchr's. guide. Human Relations Media. 2011. ISBN 978-1-55548-941-0. $149.95.
Gr 3-6–In a fast-paced and entertaining style, viewers are introduced to the MyPlate guidelines. Comparing our bodies to cars, two teen narrators explain that food and cal-

ories are fuel for our bodies. Entertaining examples demonstrate the value of eating a variety of colorful fruits and vegetables, as well as grains, proteins, and dairy products. The influence of advertising on our diets and the dangers of fast food are addressed.

ON THE WEB

All Ages

KidsHealth. kidshealth.org. The Nemours Foundation. (Accessed 6/19/14).
Easy to navigate, with sections for parents, kids, and teens, this comprehensive site provides information on a wide spectrum of health issues (physical, emotional, developmental, etc.). Games, activities, quizzes, and articles are just some of the resources provided.

Let's Move! America's Move to Raise a Healthier Generation of Kids. www.letsmove.
    gov. Let's Move. (Accessed 6/19/14).
Part of Michelle Obama's initiative to solve the problem of obesity, the site includes features for the whole family. Components include links to the White House Task Force on Childhood Obesity, healthy recipes created by young chefs, suggestions for outdoor activities, and fitness tips.

President's Council on Fitness, Sports, & Nutrition. fitness.gov. President's Council on
    Fitness, Sports & Nutrition. (Accessed 6/19/14).
Newly redesigned, the site has an appropriately stately look, with NFL quarterback Drew Brees and Olympic gymnast Dominque Dawes as Council Co-Chairs. Information about current statistics, initiatives, and the iVillage/President's Challenge (a six-week-long fitness program) can be found here.

For Parents and Educators

ChooseMyPlate.gov. www.choosemyplate.gov/. United States Department of Agri-
    culture. (Accessed 6/19/14).
Setting the standard for healthy eating, the USDA has replaced the food pyramid (though there are archived MyPyramid materials available) with the plate. Users learn about different food groups and how to fill a healthy plate. Includes printable materials and graphics.

The Edible Schoolyard Project. edibleschoolyard.org. The Edible Schoolyard Proj-
    ect. (Accessed 6/19/14).
Started by Alice Waters 16 years ago with one garden and a kitchen classroom at

a Berkeley middle school, the program has grown nationwide. Teachers will find tips for integrating food into lesson plans, and parents can learn how to be better informed about school lunches.

Eds. Note: The full version of "A Balancing Act" is available online at: http://ow.ly/yilno.

• •

—FOCUS ON—
OCEAN LIFE
Going Deep
By Kathy Piehl

Kathy Piehl is Professor Emerita at Memorial Library, Minnesota State Library, Mankato.

• •

In David Wiesner's *Flotsam*, a boy gazes across ocean swells while holding fantastic photos of undersea life where octopuses read by bioluminescent fish lamps and sea turtles swim with shell cities on their backs. Although the ocean covers more than 70 percent of Earth, most humans see little more than its surface, never suspecting how far down the waters extend or what fantastic plants and animals live there. Mountain ranges that dwarf Everest, trenches deeper than the Grand Canyon, and seafloor volcanoes exist in waters moving constantly in tides and currents. The titles listed here explore the marvels of this hidden world.

First up are introductions to ocean-related topics, including currents, tides, food chains, and topography. In *Down, Down, Down* and *Journey into the Deep*, the authors organize their tours vertically, descending into ever-darker ocean zones, revealing giant tube worms and carnivorous sponges. With thousands of animals to study, most writers concentrate on a group such as whales or octopuses to show how species interact within a habitat. Books about prehistoric ocean life allow students to compare ancient animals with current ocean dwellers, while speculation about sea monsters can turn to fact as new discoveries are made.

Challenges facing scientists remain formidable. More humans have walked on the Moon than in the Marianas Trench, 35,000 feet below the surface. Although some people dive in search of sunken ships or treasure, many more study the ocean itself. The final illustration in *Life in the Ocean*, a biography of oceanographer Sylvia Earle, shows two people looking over the water. Below them, a panorama of animals and plants extends downward against deepening shades of blue. As elementary readers dive into this collection of ocean wonders, their awareness of and appreciation for the world under the sea are sure to grow.

THE BIG PICTURE

Bang, Molly & Penny Chisholm. Ocean Sunlight: How Tiny Plants Feed the Seas. illus. by Molly Bang. Scholastic. 2012. Tr $18.99. ISBN 978-0-545-27322-0.

K–Gr 4–Sunlight's role in ocean food chains extends from surface waters to pitch-black depths. The dramatic growth of phytoplankton cascading across a spread is one of many arresting illustrations, large enough for group sharing yet complex enough to study individually. Detailed notes cover topics such as photosynthesis, marine snow, and chemosynthesis.

Cole, Joanna. The Magic School Bus on the Ocean Floor. illus. by Bruce Degen. (Magic School Bus Series). Scholastic. 1992. Tr $14.99. ISBN 978-0-59041-430-2; pap. $6.99. 978-0-59041-431-9.

Gr 1-4–A diligent lifeguard tries to rescue Ms. Frizzle's class as she drives across the beach and continental shelf into deep waters. A whirlwind tour of the ocean floor and coral reefs ends with a surfboard ride to demonstrate wave action. Cartoon illustrations and fact-filled "class report" sidebars enliven another entertaining and informative field trip. Audio and DVD versions available from Scholastic.

Jenkins, Steve. Down, Down, Down: A Journey to the Bottom of the Sea. illus. by author. Houghton Harcourt. 2009. Tr $17. ISBN 978-0-618-96636-3.

Gr 2-6–Jenkins's masterful collages reveal characteristics of animals at different ocean depths from the sunlit surface to the deepest trench. For example, contrasting images of twilight-zone animals as they would appear in light with their glowing outlines in dark water illustrate bioluminescence. Those interested in specific species will find more information after the main text.

E W Wiesner, David. Flotsam. illus. by author. Clarion. 2006. Tr $17. ISBN 978-0-618-19457-5; ebook $17. ISBN 978-0-547-75930-2.

PreS Up–Photos developed from a "Melville underwater camera" washed ashore astound the boy who discovers the device. Fantastic scenes of undersea life and images of children from years before encourage him to add his own photo to the series. Wiesner wordlessly stretches readers' imaginations about the timeless ocean circling the globe. (Caldecott 2007)

ANIMALS PAST AND PRESENT

Cyrus, Kurt. The Voyage of Turtle Rex. illus. by author. Houghton Harcourt. 2011. Tr $16.99. ISBN 978-0-547-42924-3; ebook $16.99. ISBN 978-0-547-77283-7.

K-Gr 2–A tiny turtle scuttles past *T. rex* to reach the ocean's sheltering seaweed, where she grows into a two-ton *Archelon*. Swimming with *Plesiosaurs* and escaping a massive *Mosasaur*, she eventually returns to the same beach to lay eggs for another generation. Easy-flowing narrative verse plus large illustrations encourage read-aloud visits to ancient seas.

J 597.3 Davies, Nicola. Surprising Sharks. illus. by James Croft. (Read & Wonder Series). Candlewick. 2003. pap. $6.99. ISBN 978-0-7636-2742-3.

K-Gr 3–Large diagrams and bright illustrations note the essentials of shark anatomy and how different senses help sharks find food. The fierce great white may not surprise readers, but the variety of sizes, shapes, and colors of other sharks will. Most surprising? Sharks kill about six people yearly, but humans kill millions of sharks.

Elliott, David. In the Sea. illus. by Holly Meade. Candlewick. 2012. Tr $16.99. ISBN 978-0-7636-4498-7.

K-Gr 3–Short, bouncy poems introduce ocean animals to young listeners. Evocative imagery of an octopus as an "eight-armed apparition" or a dolphin as an "acrobat with fins" plus energetic woodcut illustrations of creatures that swim, swirl, and dive across oversize pages add up to a good choice for storytimes as well as individual viewing.

Guiberson, Brenda Z. Into the Sea. illus. by Alix Berenzy. Holt. 1996. Tr $18.99. ISBN 978-0-8050-2263-6; pap. $8.99. ISBN 978-0-8050-6481-0.

Gr 2-5–From when a hatchling makes her way across the beach until she returns to lay her eggs years later, a sea turtle lives in the ocean. Pencil and gouache illustrations depict her underwater life amid sea grass refuges and fishing net dangers. Compare this contemporary reptile with Cyrus's prehistoric *Archelon*.

○ **Halfmann, Janet.** Star of the Sea: A Day in the Life of a Starfish. illus. by Joan Paley. Holt. 2011. Tr $16.99. ISBN 978-0-8050-9073-4.
K-Gr 3–Sea stars may look harmless, but hundreds of sticky tube feet under their rays, plus a stomach that extends from their mouth, make them effective predators. Collage illustrations follow a sea star's hunt for mussels and its escape from a seagull. More information, including the animal's ability to grow replacement rays, appears after the story.

○ **Markle, Sandra.** Octopuses. (Animal Prey Series). Lerner. 2007. PLB $25.26. ISBN 978-0-8225-6063-0; pap. $7.95. ISBN 978-0-8225-6066-1.
Gr 3-6–Octopuses must elude predators while seeking their own prey. Color photos reveal techniques such as blasting ink to distract pursuers or changing shape or color to blend in with the seafloor or reef. Views of octopuses from around the world will intrigue browsers and beginning researchers, who can follow the creatures' life cycle.

○ **Pfeffer, Wendy.** Life in a Coral Reef. illus. by Steve Jenkins. HarperCollins. 2009. Tr $16.99. ISBN 978-0-06-029553-0; pap. $5.99. ISBN 978-0-06-445222-9.
K-Gr 3–Coral reefs bustle with activity day and night. Paper cutout illustrations capture the vibrant hues of reef animals from tiny coral polyps to a lime-green moray eel gliding past a mucus-enclosed parrot fish. Fact pages identify coral reef locations worldwide and threats to their existence.

○ **Simon, Seymour.** Coral Reefs. HarperCollins, 2013. Tr $17.99. ISBN 978-0-06-191495-9; pap. $6.95. ISBN 978-0-06-191496-6.
Gr 2-5–Vibrant close-up photos accompany Simon's informative text. He explains how coral polyps slowly develop into colonies that form different reef structures. Careful page design matches relevant photos with introductions to various hard and soft corals and unusual reef animals. Throughout, the author stresses the importance of reefs and notes threats to their survival.

HUMAN EXPLORATIONS

○ **Becker, Helaine.** The Big Green Book of the Big Blue Sea. illus. by Willow Dawson. Kids Can. 2012. Tr $15.95. ISBN 978-1-55453-746-4; pap. $9.95. ISBN 978-1-55453-747-1.
Gr 3-6–Even students far from coastlines can participate in hands-on activities to learn

about the ocean. More than 30 simple experiments employ everyday materials to investigate topics such as currents, salinity, pollution, and camouflage. Sidebars with diagrams and photos cover current issues including environmental threats and ways to help.

○ **Berne, Jennifer.** Manfish: A Story of Jacques Cousteau. illus. by Éric Puybaret. Chronicle. 2008. Tr $16.99. ISBN 978-0-8118-6063-5.

Gr 1-4–Cousteau's childhood fascination with machines, movies, and the sea provided the foundation for his inventions and explorations that drew worldwide attention to ocean life. Blue-green backgrounds painted in acrylic on linen reinforce the watery theme, especially in the fold-out panorama of Cousteau diving ever deeper. Compare this biographical introduction with Dan Yaccarino's *The Fantastical Undersea Life of Jacques Cousteau.*

○ **Earle, Sylvia A.** Dive! My Adventures in the Deep Frontier. National Geographic. 1999. RTE $18.95. ISBN 978-0-7922-7144-4.

Gr 3-7–A marine biologist, Earle shares her lifelong passion for ocean exploration and conservation. From childhood observations of creatures on shore to journeys thousands of feet below the surface in a submersible she helped design, Earle has retained her fascination with marine life. Numerous photos document various forays under the sea.

J 627.7 **Gibbons, Gail.** Sunken Treasure. illus. by author. reprint ed. HarperCollins. 1990. (original ed. Crowell, 1988). pap. $6.99. ISBN 978-0-06-446097-2.

Gr 1-4–Gibbons's exciting account of the sinking of a Spanish galleon near Florida in 1622 and the 20-year search to locate the ship more than 300 years later demonstrates that divers search for treasure as well as marine life. Detailed illustrations accompany explanations of the work involved in discovery, salvage, and restoration.

J 551.46092 **Nivola, Claire A.** Life in the Ocean: The Story of Oceanographer Sylvia Earle. illus. by author. Farrar. 2012. Tr $17.99. ISBN 978-0-374-38068-7.

K-Gr 3–Nivola weaves quotations from Earle into her brief biography, but richly colored illustrations draw viewers on their own. Earle swims past reef fishes, walks through bamboo coral, and plunges into a galaxy of bioluminescent creatures. The final spread incorporates earlier illustrations in a panorama of a teeming world worth exploring and preserving. Audio version available from Recorded Books.

Yaccarino, Dan. The Fantastic Undersea Life of Jacques Cousteau. illus. by author. Knopf. 2009. Tr $16.99. ISBN 978-0-375-85573-3; pap. $7.99. ISBN 978-0-375-84470-6; ebook $7.99. ISBN 978-0-375-98755-7.

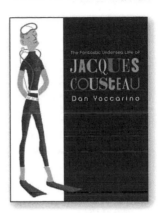

Gr 1-4–Bold colors and abstract patterns emphasize Cousteau's energetic quest to invent ways to explore the ocean, document what he saw, and share his discoveries with others. Brief quotations from Cousteau complement Yaccarino's simple text. Words are secondary to the layered illustrations, which reveal the vitality of ocean life.

MEDIA PICKS
By Phyllis Levy Mandell

Sea Turtles. By Gail Gibbons. CD. 17:38 min. with paperback book. Live Oak Media. 1999. ISBN 978-1-595-19076-5. $18.95.

Sharks. By Gail Gibbons. CD. 14 min. with paperback book. Live Oak Media. 1992. ISBN 978-1-595-19080-2. $18.95.

Whales. By Gail Gibbons. CD. 13 min. with paperback book. Live Oak Media. 1993. ISBN 978-1-595-19105-2. $18.95.

Gr 1-3–In these CD/book packages, Gibbons introduces each creature, describes its characteristics, behavior, habitat, and more. The watercolor illustrations help clarify the text. These titles are also available as multi-access eReadalongs ($29.95), which can be accessed by concurrent users.

ON THE WEB
For Students

The Colossal Squid. squid.tepapa.govt.nz. Museum of New Zealand Te Papa Tongarewa. (Accessed 6/19/14).

Gr 3-8–Developed in connection with the museum's exhibit of a colossal squid caught near Antarctica in 2007, this website includes photos and video clips that show scientists at work. Interactive features allow users to descend through ocean levels to explore the squid's habitat and learn more about its anatomy.

Marine Biology: The Living Oceans. www.amnh.org/explore/ology/marinebiology. American Museum of Natural History. (Accessed 6/19/14).

Gr 3-6–Whether students want to meet scientists, conduct simple experiments, or create art projects, they'll find modules that meet their interests. Interactive explorations of ocean food chains, sing-along tunes introducing bioluminescent animals, and conservation suggestions engage visitors in many ways.

For Teachers

Ocean Explorer. oceanexplorer.noaa.gov/forfun/creatures/welcome.html. National Oceanic and Atmospheric Administration. (Accessed 6/19/14).
 "MySubmarine" incorporates video, audio, fact sheets, and maps from NOAA expeditions into a learning adventure for K-6 students.

Ocean Portal: Find Your Blue. ocean.si.edu. Smithsonian Institution. (Accessed 6/19/14).
Photos, articles, and video clips provide extensive coverage of topics from ancient seas to contemporary explorations such as the Census of Marine Life. Users can learn about ocean features such as hydrothermal vents or view animals and plants. An educator section includes K-12 lessons and activities.

Eds. Note: The full version of "Going Deep" is available online at http://bit.ly/1ausKFO.

● ●

—FOCUS ON—
SCIENTIFIC EXPLORATION

Quantum Leaps and Bounds
By John Peters

John Peters is a Children's Literature Consultant in New York City.

● ●

L ike their Common Core counterparts in language arts and mathematics, the recently released Next Generation Science Standards (www.nextgen-science.org) are certain to fuel fresh focus on increasing students' store of basic factual knowledge while helping them acquire useful tools for critical thinking and systematic further learning. This is what science and the scientific method have always been about anyway—with the primary goal, always, of understanding the physical universe and our place in it.

The assortment of recent books surveyed below examines both historical milestones and current research that have illuminated our understanding, with explorations in two opposite (or maybe not so opposite) directions: toward the universe's smallest and most fundamental components and forces, and outward to the stars and beyond. Along with picture books that will have very young audiences thinking beyond the playpen, selected fiction and poetry are tucked into this list to demonstrate less typical but no less valid ways of introducing scientific wonders and concepts.

REAL STUFF

Primary Ingredients of the Universe

Berne, Jennifer. On a Beam of Light: A Story of Albert Einstein. illus. by Vladimir Radunsky. Chronicle. 2013. Tr $17.99. ISBN 978-0-811-87235-5; ebook $13.99. ISBN 978-1-452-11309-8.

Gr 1-3–Einstein transformed dreams of traveling on a light beam into essential discoveries about the nature of light, gravity, space, and time. In the meditative illustrations, he floats on the page, a solitary thinker pondering the universe's mysteries; more personal images of his "favorite shoes," "favorite equation" (guess!), and "favorite saggy-baggy pants" help to bring him down to Earth (and closer to mortals like us). Closing notes for older readers detail Einstein's insights and later career.

ASTRONAUTS (AND SPACE PROBES) AT WORK

Kelly, Mark. Mousetronaut: Based on a (Partially) True Story. illus. by C.F. Payne. S & S. 2012. Tr $17.99. ISBN 978-1-4424-5824-6; ebook $9.99. ISBN 978-1-4424-5832-1.

K-Gr 2–Trained with human astronauts, a small mouse named Meteor joins a space shuttle crew and rescues the mission by going where no mouse (or man) has gone before. A soaring adventure, written by a retired astronaut and illustrated in crisp, accurate detail. Fans take note: *Mousetronaut Goes to Mars* in a sequel.

Mayo, Margaret. Zoom, Rocket, Zoom! illus. by Alex Ayliffe. Walker. 2012. Tr $16.99. ISBN 978-0-802-72790-9; PLB $17.89. ISBN 978-0-802-72791-6.

PreS-Gr 1–This high-energy blend of kinetic rhyme and cut-paper collage pictures will put stars in the eyes of new and pre-readers as it introduces spacecraft from rockets and shuttles to Moon buggies. An irresistible invitation to visit the International Space Station, walk and ride on the Moon, then travel far, far beyond.

McReynolds, Linda. Eight Days Gone. illus. by Ryan O'Rourke. Charlesbridge. 2012. Tr $16.95. ISBN 978-1-580-89364-0; pap. $7.95. ISBN 978-1-58089-365-7.
K-Gr 2–"Rocket orbits./Engines fire./Toward the moon./Soaring higher." Simple rhymes and equally simple cartoon illustrations capture the drama of *Apollo 11*'s lunar mission, from liftoff to Moon walk to victory parade. For audiences who may regard that flight as ancient history, the closing author's note and photo will serve nicely as springboards to a greater understanding of a pivotal event in our exploration of space.

Silverman, Buffy. Exploring Dangers in Space: Asteroids, Space Junk, and More. (What's Amazing About Space? Series). Lerner. 2012. PLB $20.95. ISBN 978-0-761-35446-8; pap. $8.95. ISBN 978-0-7613-7882-2.
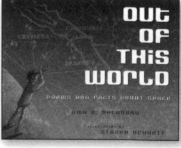
Gr 2-4–Recent news events (not to mention disaster movies) have raised awareness of the destructive potential of high-speed encounters with both natural and artificial space objects. Not that the hazards haven't always been there—just ask the dinosaurs—but this clearly written and evocatively illustrated introduction gives readers a clearer idea of just what to worry about as well as how scientists search for asteroids or other items on a collision course with our planet.

Sklansky, Amy. Out of This World: Poems and Facts About Space. illus. by Stacey Schuett. Knopf. 2012. Tr $17.99. ISBN 978-0-375-86459-9.
Gr 3-5–"The highest mountain is on Mars,/the deepest canyon too./Yet clouds of dust could stop me from admiring the view." In poetry laced with fact and supplemented by substantial prose commentary in sidebars, Sklansky presents readers with a space tour that is both informative and vividly experienced. Schuett's dark, starry illustrations add an appropriate sense of depth and distance.

Weitekamp, Margaret A. with David DeVorkin. Pluto's Secret: An Icy World's Tale of Discovery. illus. by Diane Kidd. Abrams. 2013. Tr $16.95. ISBN 978-1-419-70423-9.
Gr 2-4–Illustrated with cartoon scenes of Pluto itself literally dancing about in its

strange orbit ("Cha-cha/Cha-cha-cha") and making side comments, this lighthearted account of the search for "Planet X" is at once compelling and amusing. Besides giving due notice to one of modern astronomy's greatest discoveries, the informal illustrations and hand-lettered-style narrative add a winning sense of fun.

FAR-OUT STUFF
Wonders of Deep Space

Carson, Mary Kay. Beyond the Solar System: Exploring Galaxies, Black Holes, Alien Planets, and More: A History with 21 Activities. Chicago Review Press. 2013. pap. $18.95. ISBN 978-1-613-74544-1.

Gr 3-6–Enhancing this mind-expanding survey of our historical progress in discovering what the universe is like beyond the atmosphere, low-tech projects made with commonly available materials—from a model of the constellation Orion to a telescope—provide young dreamers and experimenters with hands-on tickets to the stars. The projects and Carson's introductions to the work of astronomers, past and present, are illustrated with a generous mix of photos, diagrams, and line drawings.

Hosford, Kate. Infinity and Me. illus. by Gabi Swiatkowska. Carolrhoda. 2012. RTE $16.95. ISBN 978-0-761-36726-0.

Gr 1-4–Looking at the stars raises a question in young Uma's mind, and by sharing that question with others and mulling their various responses, she comes not to comprehend infinity (who could?) but to reach a wise, philosophical accommodation with it. The beautiful illustrations add seemingly paradoxical (but not really) notes of intimacy, and closing comments expand on both the concept and how it is applied in science and mathematics.

Kops, Deborah. Exploring Exoplanets. (What's Amazing About Space? Series). Lerner. 2012. PLB $29.95. ISBN 978-0-761-35444-4; pap. $8.95. ISBN 978-0-7613-7878-5.

Gr 2-4–Some of the most exciting news in astronomy these days is coming from scientists who search for planets orbiting other stars—because the planets are there, and in abundance! This simple account of how those scientists work, the tools they use, and some of the dazzling discoveries they are making is illustrated with tantalizing images of what those distant worlds may look like close up.

Eds. Note: The full version of "Quantum Leaps and Bounds"
is available online at http://ow.ly/yilHO.

Sports

J

796.357 Bildner, Phil. The Unforgettable Season: The Story of Joe DiMaggio, Ted Williams and the Record-Setting Summer of '41. 32 pp. Putnam 2011. ISBN 978-0-399-25501-4. Illustrated by S. D. Schindler.

Two baseball records, both set in the 1941 season, have never been broken: Joe DiMaggio hit safely in fifty-six consecutive games and Ted Williams hit for a .406 average. Bildner, in an easy, matter-of-fact prose style, tells the men's stories in alternating sections. Schindler's ink, watercolor, and gouache illustrations are perfect for this light, affectionate glimpse of baseball history.
Sports; DiMaggio, Joe; Sports—Baseball; Williams, Ted; Biographies

J

796.323 Coy, John. Hoop Genius: How a Desperate Teacher and a Rowdy Gym Class Invented Basketball. 32 pp. Carolrhoda 2013. ISBN 978-0-7613-6617-1. Illustrated by Joe Morse.

Taking over an unruly gym class that had already run off two predecessors, James Naismith needs a game where "accuracy was more valuable than force." And so basketball is concocted. Coy's tight focus on the sport's initial season—only one point was scored in the first game—is immediately engrossing. Morse's kinetic paintings fill the spreads, capturing the game's combination of power and finesse. Bib.
Sports; Sports—Basketball; Naismith, James; Teachers; Massachusetts

○ de la Peña, Matt. A Nation's Hope: The Story of Boxing Legend Joe Louis. 40 pp. Dial 2011. ISBN 978-0-8037-3167-7. Illustrated by Kadir Nelson.

On the eve of World War II, Joe Louis squares off against formidable German Max Schmeling, a symbol of the Nazi regime. De la Peña's free-verse narrative heightens the historic sporting event's suspense. Nelson's stunning oil paintings in rich hues vividly capture not only the drama of the fight scenes but also the entire nation waiting with bated breath and quickened pulse for the outcome.
Sports; African Americans; Louis, Joe; Biographies; Sports Boxing; Nazism

Moss, Marissa. Barbed Wire Baseball. 48 pp. Abrams 2013. ISBN 978-1-4197-0521-2. Illustrated by Yuko Shimizu.

Kenichi Zenimura was known as the father of Japanese American baseball, first as a player and later a manager. But after Pearl Harbor, Zeni found himself in an internment camp, and the only way he could make the desolate place feel like home was to build a baseball field. Bold Japanese calligraphy brush-and-ink illustrations depict the painstaking work involved—and Zeni's joy at playing.

Sports; Internment camps; Japanese Americans; Sports—Baseball; Biographies; Zenimura, Kenichi

Stauffacher, Sue. Tillie the Terrible Swede: How One Woman, a Sewing Needle, and a Bicycle Changed History. 40 pp. Knopf (Random House Children's Books) 2011. ISBN

978-0-375-84442-3. LE ISBN 978-0-375-94442-0. Illustrated by Sarah McMenemy. Swedish immigrant Tillie Anderson fell in love with cycling, seeing the bicycle as a means of mobility and freedom. Placing her accomplishments within historical context, this breezy picture book biography follows Tillie's journey as she starts a physical regime and fashions an outfit of (gasp!) pants. Constant curves in McMenemy's cheery gouache, ink, and paper collage art convey a sense of motion.

Sports; Sports—Bicycles and bicycling; Gender roles; Women's rights; Women—Athletes; Swedish Americans; Anderson, Tillie; Women—Biographies; Biographies

Tavares, Matt. Becoming Babe Ruth. 40 pp. Candlewick 2013. ISBN 978-0-7636-5646-1. series.

Tavares profiles the iconic George Herman "Babe" Ruth, shining a light on the flamboyant slugger's charitable side. The author-illustrator expertly conveys Ruth's charm through mixed-media illustrations—the boyish grin, the huge appetite (one humorous scene features Ruth in front of an outlandish spread at a restaurant), the love of the game he played so well. A standout sports picture-book biography. Stats are appended. Bib.

Sports; Ruth, Babe; Sports—Baseball; Biographies

○ **Tavares, Matt.** Henry Aaron's Dream. 40 pp. Candlewick 2010. ISBN 978-0-7636-3224-3. With understated, unfussy cadences, Tavares describes young Hank Aaron's major-league dream. After a brief stint in the Negro Leagues, Aaron signed a minor-league contract with the Braves but faced brutal racism in the South. In a final illustration, Tavares's skillful combination of watercolor, ink, and pencil shows Aaron in his first major-league game. An author's note and Aaron's career stats are included. Bib.
Sports; Aaron, Hank; Sports—Baseball; African Americans; Biographies

○ **Tavares, Matt.** There Goes Ted Williams: The Greatest Hitter Who Ever Lived. 40 pp. Candlewick 2012. ISBN 978-0-7636-2789-8.

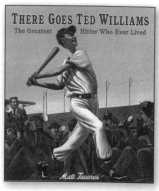

Present-tense narrative lends drama and immediacy to Tavares's all-smiles-and-heroics biography of Boston Red Sox slugger Williams. Watercolor, gouache, and pencil illustrations depict Williams as large as a double-page spread can hold. The less smiley and heroic side to Williams's character is reserved for an interesting author's note. Published in time for Fenway Park's centennial celebrations, this full-of-life biography is a hit. Bib.
Sports; Biographies; Williams, Ted; Sports—Baseball

E
V **Vernick, Audrey.** Brothers at Bat: The True Story of an Amazing All-Brother Baseball Team. 40 pp. Clarion 2012. ISBN 978-0-547-38557-0. Illustrated by Steven Salerno. The Acerras of Long Branch, New Jersey, had twelve boys and four girls. In 1938, the oldest nine boys created their own semi-pro team, which played together longer than any of the era's other (nearly thirty!) teams made up entirely of brothers. The illustrations bring the story to vivid life, while the beautifully designed pages capture the feel of this slice of American history.
Sports; Sports—Baseball; Family—Siblings; New Jersey; Biographies

J
796.357092 **Winter, Jonah.** You Never Heard of Willie Mays?! 40 pp. Random/Schwartz & Wade 2013. ISBN 978-0-375-86844-3. LE ISBN 978-0-375-96844-0. Illustrated by Terry Widener. series.
This companion to *You Never Heard of Sandy Koufax?!*, lenticular cover and all, focuses on African American baseball great Willie Mays. Readers may well feel they're at the ballpark, witnessing Mays's signature basket catches, his famous

over-the-head catch in center field, and his electrifying base stealing, all captured in Widener's dynamic acrylic illustrations. A solid, informative, and entertaining sports picture book.

Sports; Sports—Baseball; Mays, Willie; African Americans; Biographies

Wise, Bill. Silent Star: The Story of Deaf Major Leaguer William Hoy. 40 pp. Lee 2012. ISBN 978-1-60060-411-9. Illustrated by Adam Gustavson.

Wise's biography covers Hoy's whole life, including the attack of meningitis that left him deaf at age three, and celebrates the courage and determination it took for Hoy to make it to the major leagues in 1888. Oil illustrations complement the text nicely, providing historical details that will put readers in the games alongside Hoy, imagining the cheers from the stands that Hoy never heard.

Sports; Biographies; Disabilities, Physical—Deafness; Sports—Baseball; Hoy, William

* * * * *

Title Index

Author/Illustrator Index

Illustrator